the FARM TO TABLE FRENCH phrasebook

MASTER THE CULTURE, LANGUAGE AND SAVOIR FAIRE OF FRENCH CUISINE

by VICTORIA MAS

illustrated by MEERA LEE PATEL

Ulysses Press

To those who have fallen in love with,
or plan to fall in love with, French cuisine.

Published by
Ulysses Press
P.O. Box 3440
Berkeley, CA 94703
www.ulyssespress.com

ISBN: 978-1-61243-355-4
Library of Congress Catalog Number 2013957328

Printed in the United States by Bang Printing

10 9 8 7 6 5 4 3 2 1

Acquisitions editor: Keith Riegert
Project editor: Alice Riegert
Managing editor: Claire Chun
Editors: Lauren Harrison, Vincent Vichit-Vadakan
Proofreader: Renee Rutledge
Cover design: Meera Lee Patel
Interior design and layout: Jake Flaherty

Distributed by Publishers Group West

CONTENTS

ABOUT THIS BOOK

You may not have set foot in France (yet), but you're probably already familiar with such words as *baguette*, *pain au chocolat*, or *ratatouille*.

Perhaps you've sunk your teeth into a fresh croissant from your local French bakery and marveled at its perfect texture—a delicate, flaky crust with a soft, fluffy inside. Or maybe you experimented with a batch of *macarons* just to see what the rage was about, and since then your approach to pastries has never been the same. Certainly, you've enjoyed a meal at your local French *bistrot*—the one packed with customers eager to taste renowned and sought-after dishes that made the reputation of French cuisine. Whatever it is, something strikes you about this culinary world.

Whether you're going to Paris for the first time as an exchange student and wonder how you'll manage groceries or you've planned to spend your summer under the sun of the French Riviera and are eager to try out local specialties; whether you simply want to improve your cooking skills and impress friends at dinner parties with unheard-of recipes or you love French cuisine and aim to learn as much as possible about it;

whatever the reason, you can be sure you have picked up the right book.

From getting to know the typical ingredients found in a French kitchen to learning how to cook world-famous dishes; from navigating the menu at lunches in high-end restaurants or dinners in tiny brasseries; from shopping at Ladurée and Hédiard luxury shops to wending your way through loud farmers' markets: All you need to know about French food, customs, and etiquette will be found in the very pages you're reading.

By gaining insight into *what*, *how*, and *why* the French eat, you will come to appreciate a French meal to its fullest—and, perhaps, you'll become a little bit French yourself.

Notes on French Grammar

Before you bite into *steak tartare* and *fondants au chocolat*, I wish to provide you with a quick reminder of basic French. Rest assured, this isn't meant to be a thorough lesson—French language being as complex as it is—but this will give you the helpful basics to master culinary speech.

Articles

French nouns are preceded by articles, which are either masculine or feminine. From places to ingredients to objects, all things have a gender.

- "The" is translated as *le* (masculine), *la* (feminine), or *les* (plural):

The restaurant
Le restaurant (m)

The bakery
La boulangerie (f)

The Paris markets
Les marchés de Paris (pl)

- When preceding a vowel, *le* or *la* turns into an abbreviated *l'*:

    The orange
    L'orange

- "A" is translated as *un* (m) or *une* (f):

    A bar
    Un bar (m)

    A fish shop
    Une poissonnerie (f)

Sometimes you don't need an article. Maybe you just need some butter (*du beurre*) or some strawberries (*des fraises*). When this is the case, the French translation uses *du* (m), *de la* (f), *des* (pl) before the noun. For example: "I'm going to go buy bread," would be *Je vais acheter du pain.*

Bread
Du pain (m)

Jam
De la confiture (f)

Green beans
Des haricots verts (pl)

Gender

I'll always give you the two variations of a noun when they exist—masculine or feminine:

Vegetarian
Un végétarien (m), *Une végétarienne* (f)
Female nouns will usually have an "*e*" added at the end.

Pronunciation and accents

I assume you know the basic pronunciation of words after watching all of Jean-Luc Godard's movies, but just in case, here's a quick recap of the most important pronunciations:

LETTER	PRONUNCIATION	EXAMPLE English | *French*
a, à	ah	**a**vocado | *abricot* ("apricot")
c + a, o, u	kah	**c**arrot | *cassis* ("currant")
c + e, i, y; **ç**	say	**c**ity | *citron* ("lemon"), *garçon* ("waiter")
ch	sh	**sh**ampoo | *chocolat* ("chocolate")
e	euh	h**e**r | *le* ("the")
é	ay	s**ay** | *café* ("coffee")
è	eh	**e**lephant | *cuillère* ("spoon")
g + a, o, u	hard g	**g**oat | *galette* ("cake")
g + e, i, y	zh	mir**age** | *aubergine* ("eggplant")
i, î, ï	ee	f**ee**t | *cerise* ("cherry"), *dîner* ("dinner"), *maïs* ("corn")
o, ô, ö	oh	**o**pen | *orange* ("orange"), *rôti* ("roasted")
u, û, ü	eu	f**eu**d | *huîtres* ("oysters"), *brûlée* ("burned")

a: Sounds like "**a**vocado" or *abricot* ("apricot"). It's sometimes spelled "**à**" (with a grave accent) and is pronounced the same as "**ah**." À possesses many uses, such as designating places: *à la mer* ("to the sea") or *là-bas* ("over there"); or referring to a way of making a dish: *tomates à la provençale* ("tomatoes in the style of Provence"); or to describe a dish: *la soupe à l'oignon* ("onion soup").

c: Sounds like a "**k**" before -a, -o, -u, and consonants except for -h, like **c**arrot or *cassis* ("currant"); it will sound like an "**s**" before -e, -i, and -y, such as *citron* ("lemon"). For the "**c**" to sound like an "**s**" before -a, -o, and -u, a *cédille* is added and it becomes a "**ç**" like in *français* ("French").

ch: Sounds like "**sh**" in **sh**ampoo. For instance, *chocolat* ("chocolate").

e: Sounds like "**euh**" in "her." For instance, *le* ("the").

é: With the acute accent, "**é**," it is pronounced like "**ay**" in say. For instance, *café* ("coffee").

è: With the grave accent, "**è**" sounds like the first "**e**" of "**e**lephant," as in *cuillère* ("spoon").

g: Before -a, -o, -u, or consonants, the "**g**" sounds like the one in "**g**reat"; for instance, *Gruyère*. Before -e, -i, and -y, the "**g**" is like the one in "mira**g**e," such as *aubergine* ("eggplant").

i: Sounds like the vowel in "**fee**t" or "**tea**," and in *cerise* ("cherry"). Accents, as in *dîner* ("dinner") or *maïs* ("corn"), do not change the pronunciation.

o: The "o" might sometimes be spelled "ô" or "ö," but the pronunciation remains the same as "**o**pen," or *orange* ("orange") and *rôti* ("roasted").

u: Just like "i" and "o," this letter may be spelled "û" or "ü," yet it is pronounced like the "eu" in feud, like in *huîtres* ("oysters") or *brûlée* ("burned"). Remember, in order to pronounce the "u," place your lips as to pronounce "o," but instead say "e."

Tu and *vous*

The French language divides the singular pronoun "you" into two types: *tu* and *vous*.

Tu is the informal "you," used to address friends, colleagues, and family (unless you come from an aristocratic background). When getting acquainted with someone their own age, young people will usually start out using *tu* among themselves; adults will use the formal *vous* among themselves at first, but they tend to quickly use *tu* if they get along well—the French would rather leave aside formalities to get to know someone.

> **Have you heard about this restaurant?**
> *As-tu entendu parler de ce restaurant?*

Vous refers to the formal "you," used to address strangers, elders or more than one person. When going to a restaurant or a bar, you'll be using *vous* to order.

> **Have you heard about this restaurant?**
> *Avez-vous entendu parler de ce restaurant?*

In this book, I'll be using either *tu* or *vous* depending on the situation.

Of course, I can only provide a modest contribution: Your speech will truly improve when you're having a passionate conversation with the attractive stranger sitting next to you on the terrace of a café.

EATING THE FRENCH WAY

Manger à la française

When reminiscing about our childhood, we French share one common memory, an event that has become the national common denominator: Sunday family lunch.

Every child in France has experienced those Sundays when the whole family drives to the grandparents' house. The process is the same in all homes: First come the appetizers and wine—for adults, of course, although some children experience their very first taste of wine by discreetly dipping their finger in their father's glass while no one's watching. Then comes the first course, and the second; later the cheese and dessert are served.

For a child, Sunday lunch is a grueling affair—passionate debates on politics that your childhood self does not understand rule the table. It takes hours, as each family member likes to pause and talk for a few minutes before taking another bite and chewing it for another few minutes. After all, eating slowly is key to the digestive process. You keep asking if you can leave to play, but you have to learn manners and therefore must stay in your chair and listen to your elders. When coffee is eventually served, you sigh in relief as you know the end of the meal is near, yet you also know it won't be too soon. Now your parents, grandparents, uncles, and aunts are officially in digestive mode and mood, and nothing will take them off their chair for a good hour more. Only then does the expression "bored to death" really take on a whole new meaning.

Children might not consciously realize it then, but those Sunday family lunches, as painful as they seem then, are very much influential in their future attitude toward eating.

The table is a symbol of unity—a place where endless conversations take place and eating isn't rushed, as it might be during a weekday at school or at work. It is a moment when people pause and enjoy themselves while being surrounded by homemade food and the people they love. For us French, the most important meals are those that are shared. Most people love to invite their friends over and cook for the occasion. A meal reinforces friendships and forms new ones—French is a true culture of conviviality.

Food is part of social customs and holds values that have been passed from generation to generation, to the point that it's almost become a citizen itself. It is, in fact, so embedded in French culture that in 2010, UNESCO decided to name French cuisine part of the world's intangible cultural heritage. Next to the Taj Mahal and Spanish flamenco dancing, French cuisine has been acknowledged for its major role and influence on society. Needless to say, chefs all over France shed a tear of pride that day.

Chapter 1

MEALS

Les repas

To better understand French culinary culture, you need first and foremost to learn about the traditional meals: what the French eat for breakfast and why; where and when they usually have lunch, and how it is structured; how snack time in France is as relevant as teatime in England; and what a typical dinner resembles in a restaurant or within homes.

Breakfast
Le petit déjeuner

To experience French breakfast in its purest form, you must leave aside your salt shaker, frying pan, and fork: They won't be necessary. Unlike in the US or England where breakfast usually includes bacon and eggs, you will find nothing cooked or fried on a French table in the morning.

Because it's the first meal of the day, therefore eaten while trying to keep both eyes open, it has to taste sweet for the best of awakenings. *Le petit déjeuner* in France typically includes slices of bread—usually toasted—with jam and honey, croissants, yogurt, *fromage blanc*, coffee or hot chocolate, and cereal. In winter, hot beverages are favored over fruits juices and fresh fruit, which are more appropriate for warmer days.

You'll never see anyone in France quickly grabbing a cup of coffee and a croissant from a food cart while heading to work or school. Breakfast, also known as the most important meal of the day, is meant to be quietly enjoyed with your family while listening to the morning news on the radio before starting off a busy day.

Breakfast ingredients
Les ingrédients du petit déjeuner

No French breakfast is complete without bread. (Actually, no French *meal* is complete without bread.) Whether it's a packaged loaf bought at the supermarket or a fresh baguette ordered at the bakery, bread is the heart and soul of breakfast.

Bread
Du pain

Baguette
De la baguette

Slices of bread
Des tartines

Slices of bread in France are usually split baguettes.

Butter
Du beurre

What you put on your slices of bread may vary according to taste; however, most French people enjoy spreading butter on their toasted and still-warm *tartines*. In fact, jam and butter are the preferred combination to top your toast, orange and strawberry jam being the most popular choices.

Salted butter / Unsalted butter
Beurre salé / Beurre doux

Margarine
De la margarine

Jam (orange, strawberry, apricot, raspberry, mixed berries...)
De la confiture (d'orange, de fraise, d'abricot, de framboise, de fruits rouges...)

Honey
Du miel

Honey can come as a great alternative to jam, and a teaspoon in a cup of tea is always enjoyed.

Coffee
Du café

If the French and the Italian share one thing in common, it's their love for coffee (and soccer). The French know that dipping a butter-orange jam *tartine* in a cup of coffee is the best way to start the day.

Tea
Du thé

Those who don't enjoy coffee turn to tea. It may not be as popular as coffee, yet it's very much appreciated.

Hot chocolate
Du chocolat chaud

For children, or adults with childhood nostalgia, hot chocolate is among the top three breakfast beverages. Indeed, *tartines* taste as good dipped in a bowl of hot chocolate as in a cup of coffee.

Croissants
Des croissants

Croissants are usually part of breakfast during weekends. Because there isn't the rush to go to school or to work, people have time to go down to the bakery and get croissants and fresh baguettes for breakfast.

An alternative to sliced bread (or a side, why not?), cereal has become very common in French breakfast as well. It's also quicker to prepare when you've indulged in some extra time under the blanket.

Just like in the US, you'll find varied types of cereal, such as children's cereal, whole wheat cereal, oatmeal, muesli, cereals with nuts or dried fruits, and so on.

Cereal
Des céréales

You may either say *céréales* or *corn-flakes,* which is very commonly used, even for cereal varieties that aren't strictly speaking corn-flakes.

Cereal with milk
Des céréales avec du lait

White cheese
Fromage blanc

A smooth, creamy, and mild cheese that mixes perfectly with fresh fruit or cereal (instead of milk).

Yogurt
Le yaourt

EXPRESSING TASTE
EXPRIMER LE GOÛT

I'm hungry. / I'm not hungry at all. / I'm starving.
J'ai faim. / Je n'ai pas faim du tout. / Je meurs de faim.

I'm so thirsty. / I'm not very thirsty.
J'ai tellement soif. / Je n'ai pas très soif.

I love / I adore / I like to eat.
J'aime / J'adore / J'aime bien.

I don't like / I hate eating out.
Je n'aime pas / Je déteste manger au restaurant.

I find this...
Je trouve ça...

> **yummy. / delicious. / divine. / succulent.**
> *appétissant. / délicieux. / divin. / succulent.*
>
> **good. / fine. / average. / not too bad. / okay.**
> *bon. / correct. / moyen. / pas mauvais. / sans plus.*
>
> **awful. / nauseating. / disgusting. / tasteless.**
> *affreux. / à vomir. / dégoûtant. / fade.*

It's...
C'est...

> **bitter. / sour. / spicy. / strong. / flavorful.**
> *amer. / acide. / épicé. / fort. / parfumé.*
>
> **salty. / sweet. / peppery.**
> *salé. / sucré. / poivré.*

crunchy. / soft. / tender.

croustillant. / moelleux. / tendre.

It's tasty.

Ça a du goût.

It tastes like...

Ça a le même goût que...

> the dish my grandmother loves to cook.
>
> *le plat que ma grand-mère adore cuisiner.*

> real (liver) pâté when it's only vegetable pâté.
>
> *du vrai pâté alors que ce n'est que du pâté de légumes.*

I've never eaten anything so...

Je n'ai jamais mangé quelque chose d'aussi...

> rich. / copious. / heavy.
>
> *riche. / copieux. / lourd.*

> unusual. / unique / different.
>
> *singulier. / unique. / différent.*

Ordering breakfast
Commander le petit déjeuner

If you're on a trip to France, you can have breakfast either in your hotel or, better, in a café, as most of them serve breakfast in the morning. Here are some tips for ordering breakfast. Note that if you order *un café*, in France you will receive an espresso. For American-style coffee you have to order *un café américain*, *un café allongé*, or if they have it, *un café filtre*.

May I...
Puis-je...

> have a cup of coffee with some milk on the side?
> *avoir un café avec un peu de lait à côté?*

> have two croissants with jam?
> *avoir deux croissants avec de la confiture?*

> ask for another espresso?
> *vous demander un deuxième café?*

Do you have...
Auriez-vous...

> fresh-squeezed orange juice?
> *de l'orange pressée (fraîche)?*

> honey instead of jam?
> *du miel à la place de la confiture?*

> toast?
> *des tartines grillées?*

I'd like...
J'aimerais...

> a second espresso, please.
> *un deuxième café, s'il vous plaît.*

> a little more butter for my bread.
> *un peu plus de beurre pour les tartines.*

> one last croissant.
> *un dernier croissant.*

Nothing compares...
Rien ne vaut...

> **to having croissants at breakfast!**
> *des croissants au petit déjeuner!*

> **to bread dipped in a nice bowl of hot chocolate.**
> *des tartines trempées dans un bon bol de chocolat chaud.*

> **to a French breakfast!**
> *un petit déjeuner français!*

✽ Lunch
Le déjeuner

A traditional French lunch is quite a culinary experience. Ruled by an elaborate order of defined events, you may at first seem surprised by such precise ritual; however, soon you'll come to understand its ingenuity. This specific type of lunch is not an everyday habit; rather, it is enjoyed on special occasions, such as Sunday family lunch or formal lunches with business partners.

The traditional French lunch comprises five stages: starter *(l'entrée)*, main course *(le plat principal)*, cheese *(le fromage)*, dessert *(le dessert)*, and digestive *(le digestif)*. One element remains on the table throughout the whole meal: bread.

It sounds like a lot, but it actually isn't. French dishes may be filling, yet they are never overwhelming. You'll be full and content, but never nauseous. Not only are plates never overflowing with food, but sauces, fats, and butter, responsible for heavy meals, are limited in amount.

Because devoting time to eating matters, the French will rarely have lunch at their workplace (actually, the idea of eating at one's desk feels quite depressing); between noon and 2 p.m., you'll usually see restaurants, brasseries, and cafés packed with people on lunch break. Office employees are typically allowed up to an hour and a half for lunch (although they usually do not indulge in all the courses as mentioned above).

Again, eating is a sacred moment that can neither be rushed nor neglected. Here are some insights into the five stages of lunch:

Starter
L'entrée

L'entrée introduces lunch. Meant to stimulate the appetite, it's usually a small, light dish, such as a salad, soup, or vegetables. Most restaurants will help you start lunch with an onion tart, poached eggs, or even the infamous frog's legs (although, to be honest, frog's legs almost never appear on menus these days).

Main course
Le plat principal

This is typically a meat or fish. You can order such dishes as the famous *bœuf bourguignon*, the traditional *veau marengo*, the popular *poulet à l'estragon*, or the delicious *poulet basquaise*.

Cheese plate
L'assiette de fromage

Right after the main course, whether you're having lunch in a restaurant or at someone's home, you'll be presented with a cheese plate, sometimes composed of up to seven different types of cheese. The French love their cheese as much as their bread, and it's a way to start the transition to dessert.

The choice of cheeses varies according to restaurants, and they can be adapted to the dish you just had to best match its flavors. Typical cheese plates are a mix of both hard and soft cheeses; the most commonly served are Emmental, Comté, Camembert, and Roquefort. There will sometimes be some butter on the side as well.

There are certain rules to cheese plate presentation: Cheeses are to be positioned in a circle, with enough distance between each other so that they don't touch and are easy to cut and serve. They are placed clockwise according to their flavors—from mildest to strongest.

Dessert
Le dessert

If your stomach still craves for more after a salad, *coq au vin*, and several slices of Emmental and Comté, you may move on to dessert. Restaurants typically serve the traditional *crème brûlée,* the delicious *fondant au chocolat,* and the classic *tarte tatin.*

Coffee and digestive
Café et digestif

After passing through all four stages, you might need a little help digesting. The French usually end their lunch with some *liqueur* or a cup of coffee. You might think that after such meal, anyone would feel replenished and ready to go back to work, but actually, there's nothing that sounds more alluring than taking a nice post-lunch nap.

Going out for lunch
Aller déjeuner

What do you say...
Que dirais-tu...

> **we have lunch together?**
> *d'aller déjeuner ensemble?*

> **we eat at the brasserie next to my place?**
> *d'aller déjeuner à la brasserie à côté de chez moi?*

> **we get a nice steak with french fries?**
> *d'un bon steak-frites?*

I heard...
Il paraît...

> **this brasserie's cheese plate is divine.**
> *que le plateau de fromages de cette brasserie est divin.*

> **their salads aren't good at all there.**
> *que leurs salades ne sont vraiment pas bonnes là-bas.*

they make the best *tarte tatin* in town.
qu'ils font la meilleure tarte tatin de la ville.

I'd love to...
J'adorerais...

have lunch with you, but I can't today. Maybe next time?
déjeuner avec toi, mais je ne peux pas aujourd'hui. Peut-être la prochaine fois?

try out this new vegetarian restaurant.
essayer ce nouveau restaurant végétarien.

eat a large plate of mussels.
manger une énorme assiette de moules.

Let's...
Allons...

go have lunch—I'm starving.
déjeuner—je meurs de faim.

go to another brasserie for a change.
à une autre brasserie pour changer.

try and find an affordable place to eat.
trouver un endroit pas trop cher pour manger.

EXPRESSING FOOD RESTRICTIONS
EXPRIMER LES RESTRICTIONS ALIMENTAIRES

I'm...

Je suis...

> **a vegetarian. / a vegan.**
>
> *végétarien(ne). / végétalien(ne).*
>
> **on a diet.**
>
> *au régime.*
>
> **diabetic.**
>
> *diabétique.*
>
> **allergic to walnuts.**
>
> *allergique aux noix.*

I only eat...

Je mange seulement...

> **halal food. / kosher food.**
>
> *de la nourriture halal. / de la nourriture casher.*
>
> **fish on Fridays.**
>
> *du poisson le vendredi.*
>
> **organic.**
>
> *bio.*

I can't...

Je ne peux pas...

> **eat fried food or fats because of my high cholesterol.**
>
> *manger de la friture ou du gras à cause de mon cholestérol élevé.*

eat sugar because of my high blood pressure.

manger sucré à cause de mon hypertension.

eat dairy products. I'm lactose-intolerant.

manger des produits laitiers. Je suis intolérent(e) au lactose.

Beginning lunch
Commencer le déjeuner

What...
Que...

> **are you having?**
> *prends-tu?*
>
> **do you wish to eat?**
> *veux-tu manger?*
>
> **do you think of this restaurant?**
> *penses-tu de ce restaurant?*

I can't...
Je ne peux...

> **decide between chicken or beef.**
> *pas me décider entre du poulet ou du bœuf.*
>
> **eat snails or frog's legs—it's disgusting!**
> *manger ni des escargots ni des cuisses de grenouilles—c'est dégoûtant!*

afford to eat here. Look at the prices!

pas me permettre de manger ici. Regarde les prix!

Ending lunch
Finir le déjeuner

I'm...

Je...

craving chocolate cake for dessert.

meurs d'envie d'un gâteau au chocolat pour le dessert.

taking you out—my pleasure.

t'invite—tout le plaisir est pour moi.

This implies that you are picking up the tab.

quite pleased by this meal.

suis assez content(e) de ce repas.

I can't...

Je ne peux pas...

end lunch without coffee.

finir un déjeuner sans un café.

let you pay the check. Leave it to me.

te laisser payer l'addition. Laisse-la-moi.

✷ Snack
Le goûter

Just like the British have tea at 4 p.m., the French have their *goûter*. It's mostly associated with children who come home from school and have an orange juice and a piece of cake to get through their homework until dinner. However, adults who have long days of work also like to indulge in a midafternoon snack.

Le goûter, also known as *le quatre-heures* ("4 o'clock"), is usually bought at the bakery. It can be a *pain au chocolat,* a small apple tart, an *éclair au chocolat,* or even a piece of *flan.*

Would you like...
Veux-tu...

> **to have an afternoon snack?**
> *prendre un goûter?*

> **to stop by the bakery?**
> *passer par la boulangerie?*

> **a croissant or a *financier* as a snack?**
> *un croissant ou un financier pour le goûter?*

I'm craving...
Je meurs d'envie...

> **a snack.**
> *d'un goûter.*

> **a *pain au chocolat* as a snack.**
> *d'un pain au chocolat pour le goûter.*

✤Dinner
Le dîner

The French enjoy dining late, usually between 8 and 9 p.m. (although you'll often see restaurants in busy neighborhoods of big cities still packed at 11 p.m.). Traditionally, dinner is lighter than lunch, therefore meat and chicken dishes are abandoned in favor of pasta, fish, or soup. However, restaurants will offer a large choice of different meals, some as heavy as lunch. Bread and cheese are still as much part of the meal, and a mandatory glass (or bottle) of wine accompanies the meal to end the day perfectly.

In most homes, dinner happens most likely with the 8 o'clock national news on (8 p.m. being the standard news broadcast hour for most channels). It's very much part of habits to have dinner while learning about national and international news.

Going out to dinner
Aller dîner

May I...
Puis-je...

> **invite you to dinner?**
> *vous inviter à dîner?*

> **suggest this brasserie I know, on rue des Abbesses?**
> *suggérer une brasserie que je connais, rue des Abbesses?*

> **postpone dinner to tomorrow? I can't tonight.**
> *reporter le dîner à demain? Je ne peux pas ce soir.*

Is there...
Y a t-il...

> a particular place you wish to have dinner at?
> *un endroit particulier où tu voudrais dîner?*

> a restaurant that's not packed tonight?
> *un restaurant qui ne soit pas plein, ce soir?*

> a nice, quiet brasserie in the neighborhood?
> *une bonne brasserie tranquille dans le coin?*

Beginning dinner
Commencer le dîner

Is there...
Y a t-il...

> something on the menu that looks tempting?
> *quelque chose sur la carte qui te tente?*

> a way to order an appetizer already? I'm starving!
> *moyen de commander une entrée tout de suite? Je meurs de faim!*

> a better place to have dinner at than Montmartre?
> *un meilleur endroit pour dîner autre qu'à Montmartre?*

Having dinner
Dîner

Do you want...
Veux-tu...

some more bread? We almost finished the basket.
un peu plus de pain? On a presque fini la corbeille.

another glass of wine? It's really delicious.
un autre verre de vin? Il est vraiment bon.

a cheese plate? I'd like to have some cheese.
un plateau de fromage? Je prendrais bien du fromage.

Honestly...
Honnêtement...

I wasn't expecting to eat so well in this brasserie.
Look at this plate!
*je ne m'attendais pas à manger aussi bien dans cette
brasserie. Regarde cette assiette!*

I thought we would've eaten better here. Their
bread is stale.
*je pensais qu'on mangerait mieux ici. Leur pain est
rassis.*

I'm really enjoying the food.
je me régale vraiment.

Ending dinner
Finir le dîner

This is...
C'est...

the best dinner I've had in a while.
le meilleur dîner que j'ai eu depuis un moment.

the worst restaurant—such awful service!
le pire restaurant—quel mauvais service!

the first time I ordered two desserts!
la première fois que je commande deux desserts!

I'm...
Je...

going to digest for a while before ordering dessert.
vais digérer un moment avant de commander le dessert.

not sure I want to order dessert.
ne suis pas sûr(e) de vouloir commander un dessert.

not sure what I want for dessert.
n'arrive pas à choisir un dessert.

After dinner
Après le dîner

I...
Je...

thank you for inviting me.
te remercie de m'avoir invité(e).

am meeting with some friends. Care to join?
vais rejoindre des amis. Tu veux venir?

will take a cab home. How about you?
vais prendre un taxi pour rentrer. Et toi?

Chapter 2

WHERE TO EAT AND DRINK

Où manger et prendre un verre

=====

✦ The café
Le café

To experience the French way of life in its purest form, forget about climbing the Eiffel Tower or visiting Versailles—you'll rarely find a French person there. Instead, step out of your hotel and go sit in a café, also known as the second home of *les Français*.

Cafés are an important part of France's cultural heritage. In the 19th century, they were the mandatory place to frequent; businessmen to lower-class workers would duly share coffees before work and glasses of wine after work. In Paris, cafés were the symbolic place of gathering for intellectuals and artists; at cigarette-smoke filled tables, philosophers would debate social and political issues for hours, writers would pen revolutionary novels and essays, and France's young talents from the *nouvelle vague*, such as Anna Karina or Juliette Gréco, would be discovered.

Today, cafés are still very much part of French habits. You can either quickly grab an espresso before work or spend your entire morning sipping your hot chocolate while watching pedestrians in the street; you can isolate yourself in a remote booth and read your newspaper quietly or have someone meet you for an appointment.

Keep in mind, though, that you will rarely see someone with a laptop there. A café is a place you meet with your friends or colleagues to chat, where you study for a class or simply where you come to read and contemplate—it is not the place for modern technology. The French café has remained traditional in this sense, and bringing your laptop will feel odd and out of place.

All and all, a café is an authentic place for leisure, and you'll rarely meet a French person who doesn't have their own personal favorite spot.

Types of cafés

When you think of a French café, the first type that comes to mind is like Les Deux Magots or Le Café de Flore—an elegant, nice-looking café with a *terrasse* and waiters dressed in their traditional black and white outfit.

Of course, not all cafés are as fancy as the Magots and the Flore—and not as crowded either. They are regular cafés that serve beverages and meals.

Finally, you have cafés that contain PMUs (*Paris Mutuel Urbains*, state-regulated betting offices). These cafés serve coffee and sandwiches and have a counter selling cigarettes, lottery tickets, and horse racing bets. These are definitely not fancy nor pretentious, assuredly less expensive, and since they usually have a television set (electronics are usually missing in restaurants or regular cafés), you'll be able to indulge in horse races during the day and soccer matches at night.

Indoors and outdoors

One characteristic shared by French cafés is that most have an outside space with chairs and tables: *une terrasse*. If you favor the outdoors to enjoy coffee, you'll be happy to know that you may sit outside even in winter; during the cold months, cafés protect their outdoor areas with thick transparent plastic curtains and warm the patio with heating lamps. Cafés have prohibited smoking indoors, but smoking outdoors is allowed.

What to order

Cafés mainly serve, well, coffee. Most offer either Arabica or robusta varieties. Robusta has a bitter and full-flavored taste, while arabica tastes more mild and is more refined. Don't expect a choice of small, medium, large, or extra-large coffee; coffees are served in traditional small porcelain cups intended for espressos. You'll only have slightly larger cups for cappuccinos or teas. Don't think of ordering a drink to go either—the French don't drink while walking, and drinking coffee from a paper cup almost seems blasphemous.

In general, the most frequent beverages served in cafés are coffees during the day, and wine and beer at night. You may also find tea and fruit juices, as well as some cocktails (although a bar will offer you more choices of the latter). When it comes to food, cafés are less elaborate and distinguished than restaurants, making them less expensive. They serve typical, easy-to-prepare French dishes, such as *croque-monsieur, salade niçoise*, and if they cook any hot food at all, the dishes will be simple: *steak-frites*, or *moules-frites,* for example. There's also a small selection of desserts.

How to order

Just as in bars, restaurants, or brasseries, when you enter a café you may sit and wait for a well-dressed waiter to take your order, or stand at the counter and order (*au zinc*, a common practice in France, also because prices are lower if you don't sit). Tips are already included in the bill, so unless you feel incredibly generous or the waiter has been surprisingly nice to you, you may pay nothing more than the amount on the bill. Also know that you can't ask for your food to go if you haven't finished your plate. Not only is it odd, but rather impolite.

Hours

Hours vary according to cafés and districts; nevertheless, most cafés in Paris are open from early in the morning to late at night, and will close no later than midnight or 1 a.m. Cafés will close earlier in the provinces.

Coffee
Café

We French enjoy a *café* or two throughout the day. While it all depends on each and everyone's taste, a morning coffee will typically be an espresso, while a *café* after a meal or in the afternoon will vary between an espresso and a *noisette* (espresso with milk).

Coffee / A cup of coffee
Du café / Une tasse de café

Espresso
Un café

Double espresso
Un café double

Espresso topped with whipped cream
Un café viennois

Filtered or drip coffee
Un café filtre

Americano
Un café americain

Cappuccino
Un cappuccino

Latte (hot)
Un café au lait

Espresso diluted with extra water
Un café allongé

Espresso with a drop of milk
Une noisette

Coffee with steamed milk added
Un café crème

You can also simply say *un crème.*

A cold espresso topped with coffee ice cream and whipped cream
Un café Liégeois

This cold dessert is reminscent of an ice cream sundae.

Coffee beans
Des graines de café

To grind coffee beans
Moudre des graines de café

A sugar cube
Un morceau de sucre

Scalding-hot coffee
Un café brûlant

To let hot coffee cool off
Laisser le café chaud refroidir

Tea bag
Un sachet de thé

To let tea infuse for a few minutes
Laisser infuser le thé pendant quelques minutes

To take a sip
Prendre une gorgée

Waiter
Un garçon de café / Un serveur

A waiter is by definition named *un garçon de café* when you're in a café or a brasserie; at a restaurant, he's *un serveur*. You might simply want to address the waiter as *monsieur* ("sir").

Going to the café
Aller au café

Let's meet at the Soufflot café at 4 p.m.
On se donne rendez-vous au café Soufflot à seize heures.

Let's...
Allons...

> go have some coffee.
> *prendre un café.*

> go have a drink—we've had a long day.
> *prendre un verre—nous avons eu une longue journée.*

> go to this café. I know the owner well.
> *à ce café. Je connais bien le patron.*

Having coffee
Prendre un café

I...
Je...

> get a coffee here every morning before work.
> *prends un café ici chaque matin avant le travail.*

> never get tired of *café crème*.
> *ne me lasse jamais d'un café crème.*

> always have three cubes of sugar in my coffee.
> *prends toujours trois sucres dans mon café.*

I will have...
Je vais prendre...

an *allongé*, please.
un allongé, s'il vous plaît.

a coffee with some milk on the side, if possible.
un café avec un peu de lait à côté, si possible.

a hot chocolate to warm myself up!
un chocolat chaud pour me réchauffer!

Do you have…
Avez-vous…

soy milk instead of milk? I'm lactose intolerant.
*du lait de soja à la place du lait? Je suis intolérent(e)
au lactose.*

Darjeeling tea? I don't drink coffee.
du thé Darjeeling? Je ne bois pas de café.

Having a drink and eating
Prendre un verre et manger

I…
Je…

suggest you taste their Bordeaux
wine—it's quite something.
*te suggère d'essayer leur Bordeaux—
c'est quelque chose.*

wonder if they have rosé.
me demande s'ils ont du rosé.

will order snacks with our drinks.
vais commander à grignoter avec nos verres.

Could I...
Pourrais-je...

> **ask for a second glass of red wine?**
> *vous demander un deuxième verre de rouge?*

> **try your cheese plate?**
> *essayer votre assiette de fromage?*

> **get your chocolate cake?**
> *avoir votre fondant au chocolat?*

❦ The bakery
La boulangerie

One thing you're sure to find in each and every city in France, even in the remotest village lost in the countryside, is a *boulangerie* (bakery). Bakeries are at the core of French grocery-shopping habits, so much that you may sometimes find two or more bakeries on the same block. It's not a myth: The French love their baguettes. At noon and at sunset, you'll see bakeries packed with customers waiting to grab their mandatory accompaniment for lunch or dinner.

Types of bakeries

All bakeries are unique, and only you can decide which one in your neighborhood will be yours by trying them all out. However, there are also several now-famous brands who have established themselves as bakeries: *Paul, La Maison Kayser,* and *Le Grenier à Pain*. While they have quality products, they do not have the charm and the sense of familiarity you can get from a local bakery.

What to order

Bakeries, obviously, are the main provider for all types of breads. Loaves and baguettes are baked throughout the day so customers are provided fresh bread at any hour (and to avoid a shortage, as bread sells quite fast). Bakeries also sell on-the-go meals like sandwiches, quiches, and *croque-monsieur*. For snacks, bakeries specialize in *viennoiseries* (like *pain au chocolat, croissant,* and *pain viennois*) and also sell some *pâtisseries* (such as *flan, tarte,* and *gâteau*).

How to order

At a bakery, orders are solely to go. You stand in line while choosing your order, which might sometimes be difficult considering the large number of delicious-looking treats before you; you then place your order with one of the employees and pay at the register.

Hours

Bakeries open early, usually around 7 a.m. Walking by one in the early morning hours is one of the best sensory experiences you can have: a unique perfume of warm butter, melted chocolate, and baked bread takes over the street, delighting pedestrians. How, then, can you resist grabbing a croissant right out of the oven? Because they open so early, bakeries close around 8 p.m.

Types of bread: the usuals
Types de pain: les habituels

La baguette / La tradition

The famous baguette is made of wheat flour, water, table salt, and yeast or leaven; sometimes a very small quantity of gluten, soy, and wheat malt are added. Baguette's improved version is called the *tradition,* crustier, browner, and usually tastier than the classic baguette.

Le bâtard

The name indeed means "bastard." This loaf is both shorter and plumper than a baguette in shape, though the dough is often the same.

Le pain au levain

Here, sourdough is made with lightly fermented sourdough starter, making it chewier and denser than a baguette. *Le pain au levain* is made through a process of natural fermentation, composed of white flour sometimes mixed with small amounts of other flours, water, and usually some salt.

Le pain maison

This refers to the specialty of the bakery where you're buying your bread.

Le pain complet

A whole wheat loaf of bread, darker than white-flour breads.

Le pain de campagne

"Countryside bread" is a large, round loaf made from wheat mixed or not with other flours. As the name suggests, it was first mainly used in rural areas, where the cheap, large loaves of bread would feed families for weeks.

Types of bread: the specialties
Types de pains: les pains spéciaux

Le pain aux céréales

A baguette to which oats, millet, or seeds (like flax, sunflower, or poppy) are added.

Le pain de seigle

Rye bread can last for more than a week if well preserved. The best way to preserve bread is to wrap a cloth around it and place it in your microwave—when it's not in use, of course.

Le pain au sésame

A baguette with sesame seeds.

Le pain de son

Bran bread.

La fougasse

This delicious bread specialty from Provence is made with olive oil, and may sometimes include olives or other added ingredients. It's a thin leavened bread with slits and a chewiness that is not unlike a warm pretzel.

Le petit pain aux olives / aux figues / aux raisins / aux noix / aux lardons

These are typical small buns or loaves found in bakeries, either with olives, figs, raisins, walnuts, or diced bacon.

Types of pastries
Les types de viennoiseries

Les viennoiseries

Viennoiseries are the golden specialties of bakeries. These small baked goods, usually composed of butter, puff pastry, or yeast-leavened dough, are so simple yet so tasty that they always leave you wanting more. They're ideal as part of breakfast or for a snack.

Viennoiseries differ from *pâtisseries,* which are more sophisticated.

La brioche

Originating in Normandy in the 16th century, the brioche was infamously mentioned by Marie-Antoinette. It's reported that the queen, when told that the French were starving from bread shortage, had suggested to "let them eat cake". In French, the quote is actually *Qu'ils mangent de la brioche* ("Let them eat brioche"). Brioche is, however, nothing like a cake—it's a yeast dough made of flour, butter, milk, and eggs. It's perfect paired with jam.

Le pain viennois nature / au chocolat

Le pain viennois looks like a short baguette, but is tender with a soft, shiny crust. Several cuts on top shape its figure. The plain *pain viennois nature* contains sugar, milk, and butter, while the *pain viennois au chocolat* adds chocolate chips.

Le pain au lait

The *pain au lait* (milk bread) is like a brioche, containing sugar, malt, and milk; however, as the name suggests, it's in the shape of a small baguette and less puffy than a brioche.

Le chausson aux pommes

A flaky pastry, shaped like a triangle with an apple purée filling. It's a very popular after-school snack among children.

Les chouquettes

This puffed choux pastry (a pastry made from a very light dough) is covered with crusty pearls of sugar. They're listed in the plural as you usually buy them by the dozen. If you work in an office and want to befriend your colleagues, or simply set a good mood for the day, bringing in *chouquettes* in the morning is sure to put a smile on everyone's face.

Le croissant

The first croissants were sold in Paris between 1837 and 1839; who knew then that this flaky, moon-shaped puffed pastry would go on to become a culinary symbol of French cuisine? Its popularity has never decreased—a croissant is still considered the best thing at breakfast or the greatest of snacks. Bakeries usually experience croissant shortage at the end of the day, so make sure you get one early.

Le croissant aux amandes

An updated version of the croissant, the *croissant aux amandes* is stuffed with a rich almond paste filling *(frangipane)* and topped with some of the filling and almonds. Needless to say, for almond lovers, it's quite something.

La madeleine

This small and tender sponge cake shaped like a shell has made its way into the dictionary thanks to writer Marcel Proust. In his famous novel *Remembrance of Things Past*, Proust describes how the protagonist, after dipping a *madeleine* into a cup of tea, is immediately overwhelmed by childhood memories. That scene led to the expression  known today as *la madeleine de Proust:* it refers to something (an object, a place, a food) that is emotionally charged and linked to childhood. Since *madeleines* are commonly consumed by children, it is not that surprising that Proust chose this particular pastry to express nostalgia in his novel.

Le pain au chocolat

If we were to name a rival to the croissant, it would with no doubt be the *pain au chocolat*. These two pastries share the same popularity in the hearts of the French. Although similar to the croissant with its identical yeast-leavened, laminated dough and its puffy pastry texture, a *pain au chocolat* is rectangular and contains two thin bars of chocolate inside.

Le pain aux raisins
Shaped like a snail and sticky between the fingers, a *pain aux raisins* is a leavened butter pastry containing raisins and filled with *crème pâtissière*.

Going to the bakery
Aller à la boulangerie

I..
Je...

never buy bread anywhere but the bakery.
n'achète jamais de pain ailleurs qu'à la boulangerie.

am going to get a croissant. Do you want something from the bakery?
vais me prendre un croissant. Tu veux quelque chose de la boulangerie?

can't wait to try out this new bakery!
suis tellement impatient(e) d'essayer cette nouvelle boulangerie!

can't walk by a bakery and not step in.
ne peux pas passer à côté d'une boulangerie sans y entrer.

can't tell you how good this bakery is.
ne te dis pas à quel point cette boulangerie est bonne.

LE SALON DU CHOCOLAT

If you're a chocolate lover and happen to travel to Paris in fall, don't miss the annual Salon du Chocolat. Since 1995, at the end of October, this famous trade fair has been celebrating chocolate in all its glory. Around 130 chocolate makers gather to present their delicious products, while chocolate dresses strut on the fashion catwalk, chocolate art pieces are proudly exhibited, and conferences are held to talk of nothing else but the marvels of chocolate. Spin-off events are popping up in different cities in France and worldwide as well.

Ordering bread
Commander du pain

Could I have...
Pourrais-je avoir...

> **a sesame baguette?**
> *une baguette au sésame?*
>
> **an olive bread?**
> *un pain aux olives?*
>
> **a well-done *tradition*?**
> *une tradition bien cuite?*
>
> As in a nice golden brown.

a *tradition* not too overdone?
une tradition pas trop cuite?

two small olive buns?
deux petits pains aux olives?

Ordering pastries
Commander des viennoiseries

Give me...
Donnez-moi...

a dozen *chouquettes* as well.
une douzaine de chouquettes également.

this *pain au chocolat* here.
ce pain au chocolat-ci.

three coffee éclairs and three chocolate éclairs in a
paper box, please.
*trois éclairs au café et trois éclairs au chocolat dans
une boîte, s'il vous plaît.*

Ordering food to go
Commander à emporter

I'll have...
Je vais prendre...

a *croque-monsieur.*
un croque-monsieur.

a ham-and-butter sandwich.
un sandwich jambon-beurre.

two vegetarian quiches.
deux quiches végétariennes.

❋ The pastry shop
La pâtisserie

La pâtisserie (pastry shop) specializes in delicate and refined pastries. While most bakeries sell some pastries, a real *pâtisserie* offers many more choices (but generally doesn't sell bread).

Most French pastries are quite simple—don't expect to find three-inch cakes heavy with chocolate syrup and thick pies covered in whipped cream. French pastries (and French dishes in general) are about delicacy, refinement, and quality. The most seemingly bland pastry actually reveals to be unbelievably tasty, while the most gorgeous one is so perfectly shaped that you won't dare take a bite for fear of ruining it.

There is one true thing whether you go to a *boulangerie* or a *pâtisserie:* the simpler, the better.

Pastries
Pâtisseries

Le baba au rhum

This is a small yeast cake saturated in a rum-based syrup and filled with whipped or pastry cream. Invented during first half of the

18th century, it is especially enjoyed during religious celebrations such as Christmas or Easter (although you may eat it all year long).

Le canelé

This delicious specialty from Bordeaux may not appear very appealing at first. Rather tiny, shaped like a striated cylinder with a light brown color, it looks like just another tiny cake made of eggs, sugar, and milk. Don't be fooled: Under its thick, caramelized crust hides a tender, soft custard center; during the baking process, the flour is flavored with vanilla and rum, making the *canelé* a not-so-innocent pastry.

Le diplomate

Layers of sliced brioche or *génoise* (a whole-egg sponge cake) are interspersed with chopped candied fruits and soaked in an egg-and-milk mixture laced with Grand Marnier or other liqueurs before being baked. *Crème chantilly* (whipped cream) covers the ensemble.

L'éclair au chocolat / au café

You may have already heard of this famous pastry, literally meaning "lightning," Oblong, an éclair is made of choux dough filled with chocolate or coffee cream (the two flavors of this treat), and topped with icing of the same flavor. It's especially popular among children; when you walk past schools at the end of the day, you can see kids with fingers and mouths darkened by the chocolate cream of their éclairs.

Le financier

Beware of this bland-looking, rectangular-shaped pastry: Just like the *canelé*, it tastes better than it looks. Rather small and firm, with a light and moist pastry, it will enchant nut lovers as it is made of almond flour.

Le flan

A flan is composed of beaten eggs, milk, and flour, browned in the oven. It differs from the Spanish or Latin American flan in that flour makes French flan firmer and denser. It's mostly eaten as a dessert during family meals on Sundays, along with a cup of tea or coffee or as an after-school bakery treat.

Le macaron

You may already know about these colorful, round, addictive cookies. Such stores as Ladurée and Hermé have made *macarons* their specialty, and they have become famous around the world.

What is seen as the ultimate refined pastry is a confection of beaten eggs whites, confectioners' and granulated sugars, and almond flour. It's presented like a small sandwich of two cookies holding together a filling of butter cream or ganache. *Macaron* makers work on new flavor combinations every day; however, the classic *macarons* are chocolate, vanilla, strawberry, pistachio, and coffee.

Le mendiant

Meaning "beggar," the *mendiant* is an old pastry from Alsace and Franche-Comté now found throughout France. A small chocolate disk studded with nuts and dried fruits (raisins, hazelnuts, dried figs, or almonds), respectively associated with the Four Beggars, which refers to the four religious orders who took a vow of poverty and only fed themselves with walnuts, figs, almonds, and raisins. It is sold in packages containing 10 or more. They are therefore great to offer as gifts when you're invited to dinner or to congratulate someone (just make sure that the person is not allergic to chocolate or nuts).

La meringue

Composed of egg whites beaten with sugar, this dry and airy treat has been enjoyed since the 17th century. It's actually so light that it feels like eating a cloud (assuming that clouds would taste so sweet).

Le mille-feuille

Literally meaning "a thousand leaves," this pastry comprises layers of puff pastry alternating with layers of pastry cream. It is topped with powdered sugar or icing, and jam or fresh fruits may also be added. Unless you want blank stares of confusion, don't ask for it by its American name: the Napoleon.

Le Paris-Brest

This cake was named after the bicycle race from Paris to Brest in 1891; it is actually shaped like a bicycle's wheel. It's made of choux pastry and filled with praline cream and sliced almonds.

BEST CRAFTSMAN OF FRANCE
MEILLEUR OUVRIER DE FRANCE

All pastry makers dream of being named *Meilleur Ouvrier de France* (MOF)—in other words, Best Craftsman of France. *Meilleur Ouvrier de France* is a unique national award acknowledging the talents of over 100 professional trades, such as the textile industry, building, home decoration, and pastry making. The application and selection process takes years and finally, once every four years, after a strenuous three-day exam during which their skills as pastry makers are tested, six candidates are awarded this sought-after title and given a distinctive blue-white-red collar (the colors of France's flag) that grants them recognition and prestige. The president even attends the awards ceremony—yet more proof that culinary art is taken very seriously in France.

La religieuse

Invented in 1856, *la religieuse* is identical to the *éclair au chocolat*, except for the shape. Two round choux pastries are placed one on top of the other, the upper round being smaller; they are filled with pastry cream, either chocolate or coffee flavored, which keeps the two choux together. Order a pastry that has one chocolate and one coffee puff side-by-side, and you have a *divorcé*.

La tarte aux pommes

The apple pie is very famous as dessert at lunch or at teatime. You may either buy it as a whole tart for a family lunch or in individual slices to satisfy a personal craving.

La tarte tatin

The *tarte tatin* is actually an upside-down apple tart. Created by accident in the 1880s, it went on to become one of the most popular tarts eaten in France. The cooking process differs from the apple pie in that the apple is caramelized in butter and sugar before being baked. A classic dessert in restaurants, it can be served with a scoop of vanilla ice cream or with whipped cream.

❋ The bar
Le bar

A bar is the traditional place where you go to have a drink with friends. You may choose a fancy spot where ties and high heels are mandatory or a more down-to-earth bar with entertainment, such as bands playing or open mics for comedians and poets. All bars differ in practices and hours; however, most of them open around 6 p.m. for happy hour and close around 2 a.m.

Bar
Un bar

Wine bar
Un bar à vin

Happy hour
Un happy hour

A drink
Un verre

A pre-dinner drink
Un apéritif

A shot glass
Un verre à shot / Un verre à shooter

A liqueur glass
Un verre à liqueur

To have a drink
Prendre un verre

To have two drinks in a row
Boire deux verres à la suite

Alcohol
De l'alcool

Ice
Des glaçons

Bartender
Le barman

The counter
Le comptoir

Tipsy
Pompette

Drunk
Soûl (also spelled saoul) / Ivre

Let's go...
Allons...

> have a drink.
> *prendre un verre.*

> to this trendy bar I know.
> *à ce bar branché que je connais.*

> listen to a band playing live in this bar.
> *écouter jouer un groupe dans ce bar.*

Cheers!
Santé!

I'll have...
Je vais prendre...

> another shot of whiskey.
> *un autre shot de whisky.*

> just one beer. I don't feel like drinking much.
> *juste une bière. Je n'ai pas envie de boire beaucoup.*

> this cocktail—it looks great!
> *ce cocktail—il a l'air génial!*

I'm feeling...
Je me sens...

> so much better after two beers!
> *tellement mieux après deux bières!*

> a bit tipsy but not drunk.
> *un peu pompette mais pas soûl(e).*

funny. I don't think I should drink more.
bizarre. Je ne devrais pas boire plus.

great. Let's have one more shot!
super. Reprenons un shot!

Eating at a restaurant
Manger au restaurant

In any big city in France, whether it's Paris, Bordeaux, Lyon, or Nice, restaurants have rules you should know and follow. Going out to eat isn't just a culinary experience—it's a social one as well.

Dress code

Following a dress code may seem superficial, yet to the French, dressing appropriately for circumstances is part of good manners. It is advised to avoid stepping into a restaurant underdressed—sweatshirts, sweat pants, and sneakers will most likely be given the evil eye. Be careful not to overdress for the occasion either; the French never forgive a lack of subtlety.

Boots, high heels, nice blouses, and dresses always work for women; shirts and jackets are great for men. For lunch, a casual ensemble is fine, while for dinner, dress as you would for a special occasion, such as a friend's party or a first date.

How to order

Once you've sat down, you'll be given the wine list with the menu (the French know that a glass of wine always transforms a good meal into a great one).

THE BRASSERIE AND THE BISTRO
LA BRASSERIE ET LE BISTROT

The brasserie is like a laid-back version of a traditional restaurant: Less formal and cheaper, giving off a more familiar and intimate feeling, it usually serves typical French dishes, such as *steak-frites* (french fries and steak), *moules* (mussels), *choucroute* (a famous regional meal from Alsace comprising saurkraut, pork, and potatoes), salads, and cheese plates. They are open all day.

The *bistrot* is a combination of several things: It may be described as the father of the bar—while youngsters have drinks at the latter, elders go to the *bistrot*, which is cheaper and more authentic to the French spirit. Like the brasserie or the café, *bistrots* serve cheap and traditional meals as well.

After your plate has been served, don't expect the waiter to check on you regularly; he won't come if you don't ask him to. It is impolite to bother customers while they're eating, so you may sit in the restaurant for three hours without once being approached. It's up to you to let them know whether you wish to have a dessert or the check (to do so, gently raise your hand when your waiter walks by).

As at a café, the tip is already included in the bill, so you can avoid the bother of calculating the appropriate percentage to add.

Hours

Whether you're going to a fancy restaurant or a more modest one, don't aim for an early meal: The French enjoy eating late. Restaurants won't usually open before 11:30 a.m. or noon, and they'll serve lunch until 2 p.m. After this time, most restaurants close to clean and prepare for dinner, and service usually begins again around 7 p.m. Restaurants don't expect to be busy until 8 or 9 p.m., the typical peak hours; they will most probably stop serving around 10 p.m. and call it a day at about midnight.

Ordering lunch or dinner
Commander au déjeuner ou au dîner

Can I...
Puis-je...

> **have today's menu?**
> *avoir la carte du jour?*

> **have some water / some bread?**
> *avoir un peu d'eau / de pain?*

> **try the chef's special?**
> *essayer la spécialité du chef?*

Could I have the fixed price menu?
Pourrais-je avoir le menu à prix fixe?

When looking over a French menu, you'll come across two types: the regular one and the *menu à prix fixe*. The regular one is just like in the US, with many different dishes, each set at a certain price (for instance, a *salade niçoise* for 12 euros). However, the menu *à prix fixe* ("fixed-price menu"), also commonly known as *le menu du jour* ("menu of the day"), consists of just one or two full lunch or dinner meals at a fixed price, which typically includes starters, a main course, cheese, and dessert. The *menu à prix fixe* changes regularly.

Is this …
Est-ce que c'est…

> **any good?**
> *bon?*

> **hot / cold?**
> *chaud / froid?*

> **spicy?**
> *épicé?*

> **all you have?**
> *tout ce que vous avez?*

> **What is this?**
> *Qu'est-ce que c'est?*

Which wine would you recommend to go with a *blanquette de veau*?
Quel vin me conseillerez-vous pour une blanquette de veau?

Which spices do you use in this dish?
Quelles épices utilisez-vous dans ce plat?

I'd like…
J'aimerais…

to order.
commander.

a basket of bread.
une corbeille de pain.
The bread basket is always free of charge.

still water. / sparkling water. / tap water.
de l'eau plate. / de l'eau gazeuse. / une carafe d'eau.

I'll have...
Je vais prendre...

today's menu.
le menu du jour.

your seafood platter.
votre plateau de fruits de mer.

the veal stew.
la blanquette de veau.

Eating lunch or dinner
Déjeuner ou dîner

May I...
Puis-je...

have some more wine?
avoir un peu plus de vin?

ask for another knife? This one fell on the floor.
vous demander un autre couteau? Celui-ci est tombé par terre.

I'd like...
J'aimerais...

> another plate of mussels.
> *une autre assiette de moules.*

> room-temperature water.
> *de l'eau à temperature ambiante.*

Having cheese and dessert
Prendre du fromage et un dessert

Which types of cheese do you have?
Quels fromages avez-vous?

I can't resist that delicious *fondant au chocolat*.
Je ne peux pas résister à ce délicieux fondant au chocolat.

May I...
Puis-je...

> order your cheese plate?
> *commander votre assiette de fromage?*

> see the dessert menu?
> *voir la carte des desserts?*

> have two spoons? We'll share dessert.
> *avoir deux cuillères? Nous allons partager le dessert.*

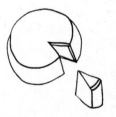

ASKING FOR DIRECTIONS OR INFORMATION
DEMANDER DES DIRECTIONS OU DES INFORMATIONS

Where...
Où...

> **is this place you told me about?**
> *est cet endroit dont tu m'as parlé?*

> **is the nearest restaurant?**
> *est le restaurant le plus proche?*

> **is Les Deux Magots located?**
> *est situé Les Deux Magots?*

> **can I go for some good wine?**
> *puis-je aller pour un bon verre de vin?*

> **can I find a nice restaurant?**
> *puis-je trouver un bon restaurant?*

Do you know...
Connaissez-vous...

> **this café?**
> *ce café?*

> **of any good restaurant nearby?**
> *un bon restaurant dans le coin?*

> **the best restaurants in town?**
> *les meilleurs restaurants de la ville?*

I'm looking for...
Je cherche...

a seafood restaurant. Where can I go?
un restaurant de fruits de mer. Où puis-je aller?

a place where they make good salads.
un endroit où ils font de bonnes salades.

Ending the meal
Fin de repas

May I...
Puis-je...

have the check, please?
avoir l'addition, s'il vous plaît?

congratulate the chef for this delicious meal?
féliciter le chef pour ce délicieux repas?

have the check yet? I asked for it ten minutes ago.
avoir l'addition maintenant? Je l'ai demandée il y a dix minutes.

Paying
Régler

Can you split this down the middle for us?
Pourriez-vous nous diviser l'addition en deux?

Shall we split the check?
On partage l'addition?

COMPLAINING
SE PLAINDRE

What kind of service is this?!
Qu'est-ce que c'est que ce service?!

Why is my soup cold?
Comment se fait-il que ma soupe soit froide?

Excuse me, this is not the dish I ordered.
Excusez-moi, ce n'est pas le plat que j'ai commandé.

I'm sorry, but I asked to leave out the dried tomatoes from the salad.
Pardon, mais j'ai demandé à ce qu'il n'y ait pas de tomates séchées dans la salade.

I would like to speak to the owner.
Je voudrais parler au patron.

It's on me.
C'est moi qui invite.

No, let me pay. I insist.
Non, laisse-moi payer. J'insiste.

Well, thank you. I'll get the next meal.
Merci beaucoup, le prochain repas c'est pour moi.

Do you take credit cards?
Vous prenez la carte de crédit?

Do you take cash only?
Vous n'acceptez que les espèces?

I don't have any cash on me. Can I pay you back next time?
Je n'ai pas de liquide sur moi. Je peux te rembourser la prochaine fois?

✺ Eating at someone's home
Manger chez quelqu'un

Going to a restaurant is great, but to the French, nothing beats a nice dinner among friends at home. If you have acquaintances in France, it's likely they'll invite you over to their place at some point. Whether it's a casual or more formal dinner, here are some tips on having the best French evening:

Don't show up too early.

You may have understood by now that the French like to dine late. Dinnertime will usually have been set around 8 p.m.; what it actually means is *after* 8 p.m.. You don't need to show up before (as the host might still be busy in the kitchen), but don't come too late, either. The best time to arrive is around 8:10.

Bring something.

The ultimate lack of manners is to arrive at someone's home empty-handed. It's customary not to ask your host what you should bring, as your gift should be unexpected. Bringing a bottle of wine or champagne, chocolates or a dessert cake is the best way to thank the person receiving you.

Avoid talking about money.

The French talk about everything—politics, arts, society, food, travels—except the one taboo: money. You'll never hear a French person mention how much they make or ask someone what their salary is—it's seen as rude. Although they might talk money-related subjects such as apartment rental prices or cost of food, they keep quiet about their own bank accounts. It's best to stick to other subjects like the latest book you've read or how you think the Mona Lisa is overrated.

Having dinner
Dîner

What did you use in this tart? It tastes great.
Qu'est-ce que tu as utilisé dans ta tarte? C'est excellent.

I love...
J'adore...

> **home-cooked dishes.**
> *les plats cuisinés maison.*
>
> **this white wine. Where did you buy it?**
> *ce vin blanc. Où l'as-tu acheté?*
>
> ***macarons*. I thought I'd bring some for dessert.**
> *les macarons. J'ai pensé que j'en apporterais comme dessert.*

Congratulations and thanks
Féliciter et remercier

You're...
Tu es...

a perfect host.
un(e) hôte(sse) parfait(e).

a very good cook.
un(e) fin(e) cuisinier(cuisinière) / un cordon bleu.

Un cordon bleu is also a typical expression to refer to a very good home cook.

Thank you...
Merci...

for inviting me. I had a great time.
de m'avoir invité(e). J'ai passé un très bon moment.

for dinner. It was exquisite.
pour le repas. C'était exquis.

GROCERY SHOPPING

Faire les courses

Now that you've tried several restaurants, brasseries, and cafés, you need to approach French food the other great way: grocery shopping. What better way is there to get familiar with French food products and learn about French shopping habits?

While strolling through supermarkets aisles, you'll experience the excitement of discovering brands that might be new to you, such as Amora, nationally famous for its pickles and mayonnaise, Andros and its acclaimed applesauce and jams, or even Président, the brand of dairy products.

Inside the luxurious Ladurée boutique, you'll be surrounded by rows of delicately colored *macarons*.

At the farmers' markets, you'll learn how to make sense of all the confusion, colors, and noise around you by getting acquainted with the vendors, tasting bread and fruits and cheese samples, learning how to stand out among the crowd and voice your order before taking a bite out of your freshly bought baguette, just like any other local.

While at the fishmonger's or the cheese maker's, you'll experience the tastiest products that will make you want to go straight for the kitchen so you can cook and eat all day.

From smelling the delightful perfumes in farmers' markets, to tasting ever so delicious specialties, to marveling at cheese stands and pastry shops, going grocery shopping in France will provide you with a unique sensory experience.

Chapter 3

SHOPPING

Les courses

There are three types of food stores in France: the tiny *supérettes*, the standard *supermarchés*, and the super stores, *grandes surfaces*. It's up to you to find which place best fits your needs. Also know that most *magasins* (supermarkets) and *supermarchés* (superstores) are closed on Sunday; instead, you can either go to a farmers' market or a *supérette*.

To run errands / go grocery shopping
Aller faire des courses

> **I need to go grocery shopping.**
> *Je dois aller faire les courses.*

> **Will you help me with the shopping?**
> *Tu peux m'aider à aller faire les courses?*

To buy some food / to pick up some food
Acheter à manger

> **Can you pick up some food on your way home?**
> *Tu peux acheter à manger sur le chemin du retour?*

> **I bought some food for dinner tonight.**
> *J'ai acheté à manger pour ce soir.*

BAGGING YOUR GROCERIES
REMPLIR SON SAC DE COURSES

There's one thing you have to prepare yourself for when going to any store in France: bagging your groceries yourself. Neither the cashier nor clerk will do this for you. Because you're on your own, remember to always put all of your groceries in your bags as the cashier has scanned your items. Otherwise, the cashier will move on to the next customer and their items will be piled up against yours.

Although most stores provide plastic bags, some stores such as Monoprix now have you pay for grocery bags (however, they are durable enough to be reused). Adopting an ecofriendly attitude is becoming more consistent in the habits of the French, so it's advised you bring your own grocery bag to the store.

Although you can find just about everything in regular markets or supermarkets, you may want to favor small produce shops for your daily fresh products. In fact, these are the most frequent places for the French to buy their fresh bread, meat, cheese, and produce vegetables.

※ The corner store
Le magasin du coin / La supérette

Your classic mom-and-pop shops, *les supérettes* are small convenience stores found everywhere in cities. They sell a bit of everything, from pasta to cleaning supplies, but they only provide the necessary minimum, so you won't have as many choices as at a regular market. They are also a bit more expensive, but when you're out of toilet paper on a Sunday, the fact that they're the only stores open in your neighborhood is really quite helpful.

※ Supermarkets
Supermarchés

These stores are about the same size as a Trader Joe's or Whole Foods in the US. They are found within cities and provide a good amount of product choices.

The most well-known *supermarchés* are the upscale Monoprix (known as the place for urban shoppers, often including prepared foods and an on-site bakery), G20 (which provides good-quality products for lower prices), and Franprix and Casino (cheap, with good products as well; great if you don't want to spend too much). Most of these stores sell the same regular, known products with prices varying slightly, as well as their own brands. (Monoprix has recently developed its own smaller version of *supérettes* called "Monop'.")

PICARD

Created in 1906, Picard has become the chain for frozen food, being the only entirely frozen foods shop. It may seem blasphemous for food lovers and cooks to not only buy but to eat frozen food; however, Picard provides quite delicious products, from appetizers such as petits fours and tiny pizzas to all types of fried potato snacks, duck breasts, soups, tarts, fish, vegetables, and ice cream. When you don't have time or feel too lazy to cook, shopping at Picard is the best alternative.

�# Super stores
Les grandes surfaces

The biggest of the three types of markets, *les grandes surfaces,* or *les hypermachés,* are the equivalent of a Walmart in size, although they don't have a drugstore. They are located just outside of town, since they are so big and French cities are usually too small to harbor them. The three major brands, Auchan, Carrefour, and Leclerc, will offer you endless aisles of condiments, cookies, and pasta. They offer attractive prices and so many choices of food that you might end up filling up your cart with a month's worth of groceries, not to mention houseware, clothes, and anything you might impulsively pick up. (Just like Monoprix, Carrefour has implemented its own *supérette*-size stores in cities called "Carrefour Market.")

※ Going shopping
Aller faire des courses

Are you going to the supermarket today? We're out of pasta.
Vas-tu au supermarché aujourd'hui? On n'a plus de pâtes.

I have to stop by the store to pick up some water.
Je dois passer au magasin acheter de l'eau.

Grocery list
La liste des courses

> **Did you make a grocery list?**
> *Tu as fait une liste des courses?*
>
> **Don't forget to add eggs to the grocery list.**
> *N'oublie pas d'ajouter des œufs à la liste des courses.*

Cart
Un caddie

Basket
Un panier

> **Let's take a basket instead of a cart. We don't have much to buy.**
>
> *Prenons un panier au lieu d'un caddie. Nous n'avons pas beaucoup à acheter.*

Item
Un article

Price
Le prix

Price tag
L'étiquette

> **I'm sorry, how much is this item? I can't find the price tag.**
>
> *Excusez-moi, combien coûte cet article? Je ne trouve pas le prix.*

Aisle
Le rayon

> **The aisles are so narrow! There isn't even enough room for two carts.**
>
> *Les rayons sont si étroits! Il n'y a même pas la place pour deux caddies.*

Coupon
Un coupon / Un bon

May I use this coupon for this item?
Je peux utiliser ce coupon pour cet article?

Cashier's counter / checkout
La caisse

Cashier
Le caissier (m) / *La caissière* (f)

To pay with cash / to pay with a card
Payer en espèces / Payer par carte

I'll pay with cash.
Je vais payer en espèces.

This checkout is credit cards only.
Cette caisse n'accepte que les cartes de crédit.

Receipt
Le reçu

I'll keep the receipt in case we need a refund.
Je vais garder le reçu au cas où on aurait besoin de se faire rembourser.

Grocery bags
Les sacs de course

I brought my own grocery bags.
J'ai apporté mes propres sacs de course.

Chapter 4

SPECIALTY STORES

Les boutiques spécialisées

You may have already heard about luxurious French brands such as Hermé or La Maison du Chocolat. These *boutiques* ("shops") were born out of a craftsman's will to make the best chocolates, the best *macarons*, or the best foie gras. Most of those brands are referred to as *maisons,* literally "houses"; the idea of craftsmanship and artistry is at their core.

While some of these boutiques have developed internationally and others have been criticized for becoming too commercial and industrial, they nevertheless still strive to provide refined,  high-quality products with an unparalleled and exquisite French touch.

La Cure Gourmande

WHEN: Established in 1989 in Provence.

WHAT: La Cure Gourmande is known for its traditional sweets from Provence. In this colorful and lively shop, chocolate bars, mellow caramels and nougats, crunchy chocolate olive lookalikes, smooth *calissons* (almond-fruit candies) and tender *navettes* (a type of cookie) will offer you an unforgettable taste of the south of France. The brand is also famous for its beautiful collectible metallic boxes, with bucolic scenes of the daily life in France during the late-19th and early-20th centuries.

WHERE: There are several locations in Paris and in different cities in France. It's so popular that it has even opened boutiques in Spain, Belgium, and the republic of Kazakhstan!

Ladurée

WHEN: *La durée* means "duration"—a well-chosen name, as the shop has been in existence since 1862, when it was first founded in Paris by Louis Ernest Ladurée.

WHAT: A luxury pastry-making house, it has made *macarons* its specialty and exported them all around the world. Ladurée prides itself in being a *fabricant de douceur*—literally, "a maker of sweetness." Nothing could define this shop better.

WHERE: You'll find several Ladurée boutiques in Paris, as well as throughout Europe and the world, including the United States.

Fauchon

WHEN: Founded in 1886 by Auguste Fauchon.

WHAT: This gourmet food company sells many products such as fine tea and quality wine, refined chocolate, delicate cookies, foie gras, and spices. Fauchon also acts as a caterer and host of dinner events. They sell such high-quality products that they have become an international reference in luxury and are admired by other businesses.

WHERE: Stores can be found all over France and have spread throughout Europe, Asia, Africa, and South America.

Mariage Frères

WHEN: Founded in 1854 and has since proven that the English do not have the monopoly on tea.

WHAT: Mariage Frères is an upscale brand specializing in tea products, from all kinds of teas and herbal infusions to tea pastries and accessories. This house of tea welcomes clients in with its colonial-inspired décor and provides service so elegant you'll definitely feel pampered.

WHERE: There are several salons in Paris and a few other cities in France. Mariage Frères have also exported themselves to the United Kingdom, Germany, and Japan.

Hédiard

WHEN: Ferdinand Hédiard began selling tropical fruits at a small stand in Paris in 1850. Today, Hédiard is among the most known and regarded brands in *épicerie fine* ("delicatessen").

WHAT: With its signature red and black stripes in the storefront making the shop recognizable anywhere, this luxury shop sells quality spices and foie gras, honey and jam, tea and coffee, wine and champagne, and mustard and other condiments.

WHERE: Many Hédiard boutiques are located within France, as well as in several countries around the world, including the United States.

Hermé

WHEN: Created in 1996 by Pierre Hermé, who was first trained by Gaston Lenôtre, then worked for Fauchon and Ladurée before establishing his own boutique.

WHAT: Because his family had been making pastries for four generations, there was hardly another path to take for Pierre Hermé. When he founded his eponymous shop, Hermé couldn't guess his *macarons* would attract tourists from all over the globe. An innovator and creator, venturing off traditional paths and marrying unexpected flavors, Pierre Hermé has become not only the master of these delicate pastries, but the true *macaron* artist—*Vogue* even named him "The Picasso of Pastry."

WHERE: Hermé's talents have seduced France—you'll find several boutiques in Paris and a few other French cities—as well as other international locations.

La Maison Berthillon

WHEN: Established in 1954 on the island of Saint-Louis in the Seine river in Paris, when the late Raymond Berthillon, owner of a hotel café, decided to make use of his ice cream maker. His ice creams quickly became popular in the neighborhood and went on to be known outside of the island.

WHAT: The most famous ice cream maker in France. Known for their motto *la qualité est notre passion* ("quality is our passion"), La Maison Berthillon takes pride in its housemade ice cream. They use no additives, sweeteners, or preservatives, only natural products: milk, cream, sugar, and eggs. Counting over 70 flavors and serving around 30 flavors each day, La Maison Berthillon is also a tea salon offering tea, coffee, and pastries. Their specialty is the *sorbet fraise des bois* (wild strawberry sorbet).

WHERE: Located on the unique Île Saint-Louis in Paris (at 31 rue saint Louis en l'île, 75004 Paris), you'll most probably see a long queue of people waiting in front any time of the day and year.

La Maison du Chocolat

WHEN: Soon after chocolate maker Robert Linxe opened his very first boutique in 1977, he was nicknamed "The Wizard of Ganache."

WHAT: "The House of Chocolate" excels in crafting all kinds of chocolate products and ravishing consumers' senses. When looking for a gift for someone or just a treat for yourself, this is indeed the best place to go.

WHERE: La Maison du Chocolat enchants chocolate lovers in France. There are several boutiques in Paris and one in Cannes. New York and New Jersey have outlets in the US and Asia. If you live elsewhere, don't worry: You can order their chocolates for any occasion as their website ships to the US, Canada, and Europe.

Lenôtre

WHEN: Pastry maker Gaston Lenôtre opened his first *pâtisserie* in 1947 close to Deauville in Normandy. Ten years later, his first boutique, Lenôtre, opened in Paris.

WHAT: Lenôtre is not your usual *pâtisserie*. Along with Fauchon and Hédiard, it counts among the top three luxurious delicatessens in France, with its array of decadent pastries, sweets, and prepared food. It also offers catering services and is a school for aspiring chefs eager to learn about refined cooking.

WHERE: Lenôtre has been delighting customers in France with several boutiques within Paris and on the outskirts of the city, and two other boutiques in the southeast of France. Lenôtre also counts several international locations.

Nicolas

WHEN: One of the oldest shop brands in France, Nicolas was founded in 1822.

WHAT: The most famous wine shop in France. Devoted to selecting, testing, and controlling their wines, as well as training their sellers to best guide and advise customers. If you are in France and looking to buy a good bottle of *vin* for dinner, you can trust Nicolas's selection of wine.

WHERE: You will find several boutiques in almost every city in France, as well as in Belgium and the United Kingdom.

Chapter 5

PRODUCE MARKETS

Les marchés

The most interesting place to do your grocery shopping is probably a produce market: Not only are the products fresh, local, and less expensive than at a supermarket, but a farmers' market is the perfect embodiment of the traditional and charming French rural spirit.

While you walk through the lively and busy rows of stalls, you'll find yourself surrounded by the loud voices of vendors appealing to customers and boasting about their products; you'll be entranced by the colorful displays of fruits and vegetables and delighted by the perfumes of fresh herbs, fish, and cheese. You won't have a choice but to engage in conversations with friendly sellers to whom fresh produce is not a job, but a passion. Wherever you are staying in France, ask where and when the closest farmers' market takes place; you can't miss out on this unique French experience.

What to expect to find

Farmers' markets provide you with all types of fresh and local products, including bread, cheese, meat, and fish, as well as fruits and vegetables. You'll also find stands selling clothes, bags, hats, jewelry, and accessories. French farmers' markets are indeed extremely rich and diverse in their offerings!

How to order

Don't pick up your vegetables yourself. Instead, wait for your turn and place your order with a vendor. They will then weigh your items one by one and determine how much one eggplant, two zucchinis, one red pepper, a large tomato, basil, garlic, and onion will cost you for your upcoming ratatouille.

Hours

If you're an early riser, you'll see farmers setting up their merchandise around 6 a.m. Farmers' markets are usually packed with people between 10 and 11 a.m. while families are shopping for lunch. The stands are taken down by 2 p.m., so be aware that farmers' markets are only open in the morning.

❊ Going to the farmers' market
Aller au marché

I'm going to the produce market this morning. Care to join me?
Je vais au marché ce matin. Tu veux venir avec moi?

I shop at the market every Wednesday and Sunday.
Je vais faire le marché tous les mercredis et dimanches.

Which days does the market operate?
Quels sont les jours du marché?

I'd really like to try this organic farmers' market.
J'aimerais vraiment essayer ce marché biologique.

Do you often shop at the farmers' market?
Tu vas souvent faire le marché?

Yes, every week.
Oui, toutes les semaines.

Yes, I never miss a market day.
Oui, je ne manque jamais un jour de marché.

At the farmers' market
Au marché

Could I taste a sample of your gingerbread?
Pourrais-je goûter un échantillon de votre pain d'épice?

This goat cheese tastes delicious. I'll have one.
Ce fromage de chèvre est délicieux. Je vais en prendre un.

Hi, can you help me out?
Bonjour, vous pouvez m'aider?

I'd like very ripe tomatoes and one avocado to eat today.

J'aimerais des tomates bien mûres et un avocat pour aujourd'hui.

Where are your oranges from?

D'où viennent vos oranges?

Their fish looks really nice.

Leur poisson a l'air très bon.

Should we go to this seller or the other one?

On va à ce vendeur-ci ou bien à l'autre?

This one looks like it has fresher products.

Celui-ci a l'air d'avoir des produits plus frais.

This one is more expensive but their meat is like nowhere else.

Celui-ci est plus cher mais sa viande est comme nulle part ailleurs.

It smells so nice everywhere; I don't know where to turn!

Ça sent tellement bon partout; je ne sais pas où donner de la tête!

Chapter 6

AT THE BUTCHER'S SHOP

Chez le boucher

═══ ❧ ═══

If you're craving fresh meat, *le boucherie* is the place to go. If you are looking for cured meats and sausages, you want a *charcuterie*.

- *Le boucher* is actually the name of the profession (the butcher).

- *La boucherie* is the name of the shop. It sells all kinds of meat, mainly beef, pork, and poultry.

- *La charcuterie* is the shop specializing in cured or prepared pork products, selling notably ham, pâtés, and sausages.

- *Le charcutier* is the name of the profession. A *boucher* can be a *charcutier* as well.

Butcher / Cured meat butcher
Le boucher / Le charcutier

Butcher's shop / Cured meat shop and delicatessen
La boucherie / La charcuterie

Poultry seller (exclusively selling poultry)
Un volailler

We're going...
Nous allons...

> **to the delicatessen.**
> *chez le charcutier. / à la charcuterie.*

> **to the butcher's shop.**
> *chez le boucher / à la boucherie.*

❧ Beef
Le bœuf

Cuts of beef in the US and France differ so I've used the closest English translations. If you really must have a particular US cut, it would be best to point out exactly what part of the cow you mean on a beef chart.

Beef shank / Brisket
Le jarret / La poitrine de boeuf
BEST PREPARED: For stews. *Jarret de bœuf* is a classic cut of meat found in various recipes, such as with tomato sauce or lentils.

Beef cutlet
L'escalope de bœuf
BEST PREPARED: Grilled or baked. *Escalope de bœuf* is a beef cut; However veal cutlet (*escalope de veau*) is more popular.

Hanging tender
Le tendron

BEST PREPARED: Stir-fried, stewed, or grilled. Veal (*tendron de veau*) is more commonly consumed than beef (*tendron de bœuf*).

Hanger steak
L'onglet de bœuf
BEST PREPARED: Marinated and grilled.

Beef tongue
La langue de bœuf
BEST PREPARED: Boiled. *Langue de bœuf* is usually served in thick, spicy sauces.

Chuck steak
Le paleron
BEST PREPARED: Braised, stewed, or roasted. Usually cooked and served with vegetables, especially carrots.

Flank steak
La bavette
BEST PREPARED: Grilled, pan-fried, braised, or broiled.

Ground beef
Du steak haché
BEST PREPARED: Raw, grilled, or roasted. If you order *steak haché* in France, it will most likely be served with french fries.

Sirloin steak
Un rumsteck
BEST PREPARED: Grilled or pan-fried.

Sirloin steak (cut closer to the ribs)
Un faux-filet
BEST PREPARED: Grilled, roasted, or pan-fried.

Rib-eye steak (bone-in)
La côte de bœuf
BEST PREPARED: Grilled or barbecued.

Rib roast
Plat de côtes
BEST PREPARED: Stewed or braised. *Pot-au-feu* is a typical French stew that is made quite tastily with this cut of beef, along with several other cuts.

Rib steak
L'entrecôte
BEST PREPARED: Grilled or pan-fried. It makes a great dish with potatoes or green vegetables.

Roast beef
Le rôti de bœuf
BEST PREPARED: Roasted. *Rôti de bœuf* is a dish itself, served with french fries, potatoes, or vegetables.

Shoulder blade
Une macreuse
BEST PREPARED: Stewed, grilled, or fried. A popular dish with mashed potatoes.

Beef cheek
La joue
BEST PREPARED: Braised or *bourguignon*-style (stewed). Often served with carrots.

Rumpsteak
La tranche de boeuf
BEST PREPARED: Roasted.

Beef tenderloin
Le filet de bœuf
BEST PREPARED: Grilled or skillet-roasted.

Round
La gîte à la noix
BEST PREPARED: Braised or roasted.

Pork
Le porc

Pork tenderloin
Le filet mignon de porc
BEST PREPARED: Pan-fried, grilled, or braised. This refers to the most tender part of the pork in the posterior region. Remember, in France "filet mignon" refers to pork and in the US to beef.

Ground pork
Du porc haché
BEST PREPARED: Fried, in pâtés and meatballs.

Ham shank
Le jambonneau (small ham)
BEST PREPARED: As is (usually sold cured or brined and pre-cooked) or roasted. Usually served with lentils.

Pork loin
La longe
BEST PREPARED: Grilled or roasted.

Pork belly
La poitrine de porc
BEST PREPARED: Marinated and
braised.

Pork chops
Les côtes de porc
BEST PREPARED: Grilled,
roasted, fried, or slowly cooked.

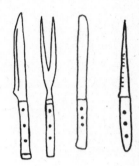

Picnic shoulder
L'épaule
BEST PREPARED: Roasted or braised.

Shoulder butt (or shoulder roast)
La palette
BEST PREPARED: As is (if it comes brined), roasted, or
grilled. The dish is usually served with vegetables and
potatoes.

Sirloin
Un filet de porc
BEST PREPARED: Grilled, roasted, or fried. Typically served
with french fries.

Spare ribs
Les travers
BEST PREPARED: Grilled, roasted, or braised.

❈ Chicken and poultry
Poulet et volaille

Chicken breast
Du blanc de poulet
BEST PREPARED: Grilled,
roasted, or cooked with sauce.

Chicken drumstick
Un pilon de poulet
BEST PREPARED: Marinated and roasted.

Chicken thigh
La cuisse de poulet
BEST PREPARED: Broiled, fried, or slow-cooked. Usually
served with potatoes. On a menu, *cuisse* refers to the whole
leg.

Chicken heart
Des cœurs de poulet
BEST PREPARED: Grilled or pan-fried. It is, however,
not a very conventional dish to be cooked or served in
restaurants.

Chicken wing
L'aile / Le manchon de poulet
BEST PREPARED: Grilled, fried, or roasted.

Depending on butcher shops, you may also find:

Turkey
De la dinde

Rabbit
Du lapin

Duck
Du canard

Hare
Du lièvre

Hen
Du coq

Lamb
De l'agneau

And more rarely:

Boar
Du sanglier

Pheasant
Du faisan

Quail
Des cailles

※Cured meats and other specialties
La charcuterie et d'autres spécialités

Ham
Du jambon

BEST PREPARED: Cured, braised, grilled, or roasted. Ham in France is mostly consumed in the popular *sandwich jambon-beurre,* baguette sandwiches with ham and butter. You can purchase either *jambon cru* (cured and air-dried like prosciutto) or *jambon blanc* (cured and boiled).

Salami
Le saucisson

One of the major culinary symbols of France, the *saucisson* has been a favorite of the French for centuries. This dry, cured, and seasoned sausage is a mandatory offering at picnics or Sunday lunches. The French like it best in sandwiches, with pickles and butter.

Sausage
La saucisse

Sausage comes in many shapes and tastes according to regions. Depending on where you're staying in France, you may come across the *saucisse aux herbes, saucisse de Strasbourg, saucisse de*

Toulouse, and so on. The French particularly like their *saucisse* with mashed potatoes.

Boudin sausage
Le boudin

Le boudin is a type of pork sausage made with fresh whole eggs and milk. The most commonly found and bought is the *boudin blanc* (white *boudin*). You may also find *boudin noir* (black *boudin*), which is a blood sausage containing pork meat and blood.

Be careful, as *boudin* is also a derogatory term to refer to a not-so-thin girl.

Andouille sausage
L'andouille

A smoked sausage made from the pork's intestines and stomach, it traditionally has a long shape (usually nine inches) and is quite thick, although its size may vary by region. *Andouille* is also slang for "dumb" or "idiot." It is cold cut and served sliced. They are quite pungent and are not what you might anticipate a Cajun-style andouille to be like.

Andouillette sausage
L'andouillette

The *andouillette* consists of pork gut stuffed with pork intestines previously cooked with spices and condiments such as mustard.

Foie gras
Le foie gras / La terrine de foie gras

Most French refrigerators will always have one or two cans or jars of foie gras,

fattened duck or goose liver. After all, France is the leading producer of foie gras in the world, as well as the leading consumer.

Pork shoulder rillettes
Les rillettes de porc

Les rillettes de porc is pork meat chopped and cooked in fat. Only salt and pepper are used for seasoning. While pork is the most famous of all *rillettes*, you may also find *rillettes* of duck, rabbit, goose, salmon, or tuna. *Les rillettes de porc* are mostly used in sandwiches.

Paupiettes
La paupiette

This thin piece of meat, usually beef or veal, is stuffed with vegetables then rolled and sold as is, to be braised at home. Its name in Provence is *alouette sans tête* ("headless lark").

Tripe
Les tripes

Tripe is organ meat from farm animals' stomachs (usually beef, but also sheep). Butchers sell it already blanched and ready to add to the dish of your choice, saving you hours of prep time. The *andouille* and the *andouillette* sausages contain *tripes*.

La crépinette

Often defined as a flat sausage, the *crépinette* is chopped meat locked in *crépine* (caul fat), which is then flattened. It is usually eaten as an hors d'oeuvre.

La galantine

To make a *galantine*, meat is poached, coated with gelatin, and served cold. With its cylindrical shape, the *galantine* comes in many forms of meat: poultry, duck, pheasant, young wild boar, or lamb.

PÂTÉ
PÂTÉ

A mixture of ground meat and minced fat, eggs, and spices, *pâté* takes on many roles: It can be spread on slices of bread to make the best sandwiches for lunch; it can be used as a stuffing for tarts or flaky pastries; and it's also a necessary part of feasts, such as Christmas Eve dinner.

You can find different types of *pâté*:

- *le pâté en croûte* (baked in crust like a tart);
- *le pâté de sanglier* (wild boar pâté);
- *pâté de saumon* (salmon pâté).
- *pâté de foie gras* is a normal meat pâté enriched with the addition of fattened liver, usually of duck.

In Paris, Foie Gras et Confits and Lafitte shops specialize in all types of quality foie gras products.

❋ Meat pastries
Charcuterie pâtissière

Some *boucheries* and *charcuteries* also provide catering services and sell meat pastries with cheese and/or vegetables. Here are the most common:

La bouchée à la reine

Originally from Lorraine, this is a small and round flaky pastry filled with mushrooms and poultry or veal bits. It is called *vol-au-vent* when its size is slightly larger (about three inches).

La quiche

A quiche is the most popular savory tart in France. These flaky pastries are found in many different flavors, although the most famous one, *quiche lorraine*, is made with cubed slab bacon, eggs, and cream or milk. It can also be found in bakeries.

Le croque-monsieur

Croque comes from the verb *croquer*, meaning "to munch." One of the simplest yet most common sandwiches in France, it's sold in bakeries, delicatessens, and charcuteries, as well as served in brasseries and cafés. This toasted sandwich is made with the preferred French combination: ham and cheese.

Le croque-madame

The feminine version of the *croque-monsieur* only differs in that it has a fried egg on top.

Le friand

A flaky pastry usually made with ham and cheese, it is eaten as a starter or an appetizer. The expression *être friand de quelque chose* means to be fond of some type of food so a *friand* is literally something of a treat!

I'm fond of beef tongue.
Je suis friand(e) de la langue de bœuf.

✾ Inquiring
Demander

Are your chickens free range?
Vos poulets sont-ils élevés en plein air?

Where do your meats come from?
D'où proviennent vos viandes?

Are you assuring me no growth hormones were used in your meats?
Vous me certifiez qu'aucune hormone de croissance n'a été utilisée dans vos viandes?

What is this?
Qu'est-ce que c'est?

How much do you think I will need to feed four people?
Combien pensez-vous qu'il me faut pour quatre personnes?

Do you sell hare?
Vous vendez du lièvre?

Do you have boneless chicken breast?
Auriez-vous du blanc de poulet désossé?

I prefer bone-in chicken legs.
Je préfère les cuisses de poulet avec l'os.

✺ Ordering
Commander

I'd like...
Je voudrais...

> three slices of ham, please.
> *trois tranches de jambon, s'il vous plaît.*

> a can of your best foie gras.
> *une boîte de votre meilleur foie gras.*

> some andouille and some lard.
> *un peu d'andouille et du lard.*

> two pounds of *boudin blanc*.
> *un kilo de boudin blanc.*

> a half-pound of chicken breast.
> *250 grammes de blancs de poulet.*

Give me...
Donnez-moi...

one free-range chicken, well roasted.
un poulet fermier bien rôti.

this nice rib steak there.
cette belle entrecôte-ci.

some *rillettes de porc*, too.
des rillettes de porc en plus.

Chapter 7

AT THE FISHMONGER'S

Chez le poissonnier

If you walk the streets of any French city early in the morning, you'll see fishmongers busy preparing their fish long before the light of day has struck the streets.

Fishmonger
Le poissonnier

Seafood shop
La poissonnerie

We're going...
Nous allons...

> **to the fishmonger's.**
> *chez le poissonnier.*

> **to the fish shop.**
> *à la poissonnerie.*

Seafood / Seafood platter
Les fruits de mers / Le plateau de fruits de mer

Seafood platters on crushed ice include mollusks and shellfish, but not fin fish.

✳ Major fish families
Les grandes familles de poissons

Alaska pollock
Le colin

Best poached, fried, or au gratin. People usually eat a *filet de colin* paired with vegetables or rice.

Anchovy
L'anchois

Usually served as an appetizer or baked in tarts. The most common anchovy is the European anchovy (*l'anchois européen*).

Atlantic herring
Le hareng

You can buy *hareng frais* ("fresh herring"), *hareng fumé* ("smoked herring"), *hareng salé* ("salted herring"), *hareng mariné* ("marinated herring"), or *hareng saur* ("salted and smoked herring").

Carp
La carpe

Carp can be grilled, roasted, braised, or stuffed. It can also be cooked *en matelote*, meaning that the fish is cooked in white wine or sometimes beer.

Cod
Le cabillaud

While the *cabillaud* is the fish itself, salt cod is called *morue*; cod liver oil is called *huile de foie de morue*.

In slang, *une morue* is a derogatory term to refer to a woman with low morals. Cod can be braised, steamed, roasted, or fried, and is typically paired with mustard or cream.

Eel
L'anguille

Smoked eel with lemon is served as an appetizer. Fresh, it can also be marinated, poached, or stewed.

Halibut
Le flétan

Popular for its delicate taste, halibut is usually ready-smoked then braised.

Mackerel
Le maquereau

There exist many different types of *maquerau*: *maquereau atlantique*, *maquereau bley*, and *maquereau commun*. It tastes best marinated then grilled, and is ideally paired with white wine and green vegetables.

Monkfish/Lotte
La lotte de rivière

A codlike river fish. Not to be confused with *la lotte*, which refers to another fish. *Filet de lotte* is a popular dish that's usually fried.

Northern pike
Le brochet

Usually served broiled, fried, or stuffed.

Salmon
Le saumon

Can be bought already smoked *(saumon fumé)*, or fresh to be braised, fried, poached, or cooked in sauce. Salmon steak is usually ordered as *pavé de saumon* (bone-in) or as *filet de saumon* (fillet). Smoked salmon is served as an appetizer, while cooked salmon is typically served with white rice.

Sardine
La sardine

Mostly sold in cans. But fresh they also taste great grilled, braised, stuffed, or fried.

Skate
La raie

Served pan-fried with butter and capers.

Sole
La sole

La sole meunière is a typical dish served in France in which sole is floured on both sides before being fried and then served with minced parsley, lemon, and browned butter on top.

Sturgeon
L'esturgeon

Probably one of the most sought-after fishes, as sturgeon eggs are used to produce caviar. The fish itself also boasts a tender and tasty flesh, devoid of bones, that can be braised, fried, grilled, or roasted.

Swordfish
L'espadon

Once you've bought your swordfish steak or fillet at your local fishmonger's, you may grill, roast, fry, or even smoke it. Infuse it with herbs such as rosemary or thyme, and serve it with pasta.

Trout
La truite

Braised or fried, trout fillet *(filet de truite)* is a popular dish in France that people like to order in restaurants or cook at home, as it is quite easy to cook. It's usually served sautéed with shallots.

Tuna
Le thon

Canned or fresh, bakeries sell tuna sandwiches, while restaurants will serve *salade niçoise*, in which tuna is one of the major components.

Whiting
Le merlan

A codlike fish, whiting is usually floured and then braised, fried, grilled, or poached in wine and paired with vegetables and potatoes.

There's a funny, popular expression *avoir des yeux de merlan frit* ("to have fried whiting eyes"), which refers to someone in love having a naive, almost idiotic look in their eyes.

❋ Shellfish
Les crustacés

Crab
Le crabe

Crab requires a very simple cooking technique: Place a live crab in salted boiling water. Let it cook for 15 to 20 minutes, then you're done! In the Mediterranean region, the *crabe de roche* (also known as *crabe vert*) is a component of traditional southern recipes such as fish soup.

Lobster
Homard

Considered one of the finest types of shellfish. Just like crab, it is best boiled or steamed, and served with butter, garlic, lemon, or mayonnaise.

Shrimp
La crevette

Shrimp, peeled and deveined, are usually cooked in boiling salted water. They are often served cold as appetizers *(hors-d'oeuvre)*, alongside mayonnaise, avocado, or tomatoes. They also can be prepared in a sauce, such as in Marseille where shrimp is sautéed in dry white wine, cream, and aniseed.

Spiny lobster
La langouste

Its delicious tail flesh makes for a fine meal, whether it's broiled, boiled, or fried.

Clam
La palourde / La praire

Les palourdes farcies ("stuffed clams") are a typical French dish in which clams are cooked and then topped with snail butter *(beurre d'escargot)*. Don't worry, snail butter isn't actually snail mixed with butter: It's simply a type of butter prepared with shallots, parsley, garlic, and black pepper.

King scallop
La coquille Saint Jacques

Considered a refined item and dish by many. Not to be confused with *pétoncles,* which refers to bay scallops. King scallops are usually pan-fried or broiled on the half-shell.

Mussels
Les moules

The always-popular mussels are traditionally cooked with butter and white wine and served with french fries.

Oyster
L'huître

Oysters are mostly eaten at the end of the year, for Christmas or New Year's Eve, and are usually served as part of a platter of seafood. Best raw, with lemon juice or shallot vinegar, known as *sauce mignonette*.

Sea snail (winkle)
Le bigorneau

You're likely to find sea snails as part of seafood platters served in restaurants. If you intend on making some at home, disgorge them in salt water for 24 hours, boil them and enjoy with buttered bread.

Octopus
Le poulpe

Typically grilled or stewed.

Squid
Le calmar / Le calamar

Except for the beak and pen (a hard internal body part), the whole squid is edible. It has to be cooked over low heat or quickly deep-fried.

✺Other selections from the fishmonger
Autres sélections du poissonnier

Imitation crab
Le surimi

France is the top European consumer of surimi. These are small and tender batons made from the flesh of white fish such as whiting or Alaska pollock.

Sea urchin
L'oursin

You can buy fresh sea urchins at the fish shop or in cans in supermarkets.

Snails
Les escargots

Typical of French cuisine, snails might either appeal to you or plain repel you. Snails are usually broiled or braised, and garnished with parsley butter and garlic.

✳ Inquiring
Demander

Which are your boneless fishes?
Quels sont vos poissons sans arêtes?

Which fish do you recommend to go along with potatoes?
Quel poisson me recommandez-vous pour accompagner un plat des pommes de terre?

Do you sell octopus?
Vous vendez du poulpe?

Are your fish farm-raised?
Vos poissons sont-ils des poissons d'élevage?

Are your fish wild?
Vos poissons sont-ils des poissons sauvages?

Are your fish fresh?
Vos poissons sont-ils frais?

Were your fish previously frozen?
Vos poissons ont-ils été surgelés?

Which fish do you recommend to hold up in a stew?
Quel poisson me recommandez-vous pour un plat mijoté?

Which types of caviar do you have?
Quels types de caviar avez-vous?

※ Ordering
Commander

Could I get...
Pourrais-je avoir...

> **three fresh salmon steaks?**
> *trois pavés de saumon frais?*

> **a dozen oysters?**
> *une douzaine d'huîtres?*

> **two cans of tuna?**
> *deux boîtes de thon?*

> **two pounds of scallops, please.**
> *un kilo de coquilles saint Jacques, s'il vous plaît.*

I would like...
J'aimerais...

> **your best sole.**
> *votre meilleure sole.*

> **shrimp for four.**
> *des crevettes pour quatres personnes.*

> **the same cod as usual.**
> *le même cabillaud que d'habitude.*

Chapter 8

AT THE CHEESE SHOP

Chez le fromager

Often nicknamed "the land of cheese," it's difficult for France to deny that moniker: There's hardly another place in the world where you can find as many cheeses, and as delicious.

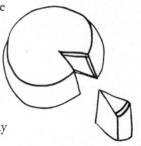

The leading exporter of cheese in the world as well as an intense consumer, France produces more than 300 types of cheese, which are divided into families according to their structure and crust. Cheese even has its own National Cheese Day on March 29.

And cheese isn't just a popular food: It's embedded in French custom and culture. A traditional French meal inevitably includes cheese; anyone having family or friends over will offer them cheese (usually at the end of the meal); and an ideal sandwich will invariably include cheese.

Cheese is everywhere—any moment of the meal, any time of the day.

It may seem cliché to declare that no cheeses are alike, but this statement applies perfectly to French cheeses. Each cheese has a unique story that distinguishes it from others and places it in a particular place in France's culinary history. Each and every one possesses its own defining characteristics that will determine how, when, and with what it will be paired. Because so many criteria and details define the identity of each cheese, we can hardly neglect the value and significance cheeses hold.

The cheese shop *(la fromagerie)* will provide you with the most popular French cheeses (Camembert, chèvre, Emmental, Comté, Cantal, and so on), other common cheeses, as well as some you may never have heard of. When purchasing cheeses, for quality purposes, make sure to note that oftentimes there is an industrial or farm-fresh version of the cheese. The farm-produced variety *(fermier)* and the kind made by industrial dairy companies will appear identical. To distinguish the two, look at the marking: farm-produced cheeses display an elliptical badge imprinted with the name of the farm and the word "*fermier*"; for example, "Saint-Nectaire Fermier" (traditionally made by farmers in Saint-Nectaire) in tall, black letters. It's also inscribed with the registration number of the artisan producer. *La fromagerie* will also offer you its own cheese creations, such as goat cheese covered with dried fruits or nuts, for instance. Note that a cheese shop will also sell fresh eggs (oddly enough, it usually doesn't sell milk).

AOC
AOC

While looking at the different types of cheeses on display, you may notice a little red label with the letters: AOC (*Appellation d'Origine Contrôlée*, or "Certified Designation of Origin").

Around 40 types of cheese in France possess this official label that protects their name by guaranteeing their geographical origins and assessing their traditional process of fabrication.

The AOC label also applies to a wide range of products such as: wine, fruits, vegetables, milk, and honey.

Along with AOC you may also find another similar label, AOP (*Appellation d'Origine Protégée*), which translates as "Protected Designation of Origin." This is not a French but a European identification that protects the name and origin of some products.

Cheese maker (or vendor)
Le fromager

Cheese maker
L'affineur
One who ages the cheeses as well.

Cheese shop
La fromagerie

We are going...
Nous allons...

> **to the cheese maker's.**
> *chez le fromager.*

> **to the cheese shop.**
> *à la fromagerie.*

Where is the nearest cheese shop?
Où est la fromagerie la plus proche?

Because we would have to dedicate a whole other book to cheese in order to name the 300 types that exist, here are the most significant families:

- **Hard cheeses:** Cow or ewe milk. Wheel-like shape, yellow color, and firm rind. Includes Comté, Emmental, and Morbier.

- **Soft cheeses:** Cow, ewe, or goat milk. Prominent white color. Supple texture and taste. Includes Camembert, Reblochon, and Crottin de Chavignol.

- **Fresh curd cheese and processed cheeses:** Cow, ewe, or goat milk. Young, mellow, and creamy. White colored. Includes Cancoillote, Caillebotte, and fromage blanc.

- **Blue-veined cheeses:** Cow, ewe, or goat milk. Varies from blue to green to gray stains. Very strong and spicy flavor. Includes Bleu d'Auvergne and Roquefort.

Just like wine, cheese is often named after the region it's made in. To enjoy cheese to the best of its taste, it's advised to take it out of the fridge an hour before consuming it.

Hard cheeses
Fromages à pâte pressée

This is the first great family of cheeses. During the cheese-making process, milk undergoes curdling and forms a curd (the solid part of milk). The curd is then pressed before being placed into molds to adapt to the desired shape of the cheese, then it is drained. Compared to other types of cheeses, hard cheeses require an intense and longer curdling and draining process. There are two types of hard cheeses: uncooked and cooked.

Uncooked, pressed cheeses
Fromages à pâte pressée non cuite

For these particular cheeses, curd undergoes a lower heating process, never reaching over 122°F. Curd may also be pressed after molding. Depending on the length of the pressing process, the moisture level of the paste will vary. Maturing can last from three weeks up to a year.

Le Beaumont

ORIGINS: Created in the mountains of Haute-Savoie in 1881, this flat, disk-shaped cheese is made from pasteurized cow milk.

PROCESS: Measuring around 1.5 by 8 inches and weighing an average 3.3 pounds, it takes a month and a half for this cheese to mature.

FLAVOR: Sweet and creamy.

PAIRING: Usually eaten at the end of meals, along with white wine.

Le Cantal

ORIGINS: This famous, cylindrical cheese was born in the valleys of the Massif Central in 1298.

PROCESS: Made from pasteurized or raw cow milk, it demands 33 hours of preparation and a minimum of 30 days of maturation for a "young" Cantal, and 240 days for an "old" Cantal.

FLAVOR: Depending on its ripeness, it ranges from supple to firm, and it has a milky to nutty flavor.

PAIRING: Cantal is used for many recipes, ranging from poached eggs to tarts to even muffins.

Le Mont-des-Cats

ORIGINS: Created in the 19th century by the Trappist monks of the abbey of Port du Salut. Today, this cheese is still made entirely by hand by the monks of the monastery, thereby expressing the true definition of craftsmanship.

PROCESS: Maturation lasts for a month, during which the cheese is washed with brine, which gives it its ginger color.

FLAVOR: Unlike other cheeses, it hardly has any odor and possesses a very light flavor.

PAIRING: Great match with red wine like a light Loire.

Le Morbier

ORIGINS: Ever since the 19th century, Morbier was made in the small town of the same name in the region of Jura, located at an altitude of more than 2,000 feet.

Morbier was born from Comté (a distant cousin of Gruyère) leftovers; when there wasn't enough milk left to make another Comté, farmers would keep the remaining milk in a tank. The surface was coated with ash scraped from a cooking pot to keep insects away at night. Farmers would then cover the surface with another layer of milk; and as the cheese set, a dark line from the ash coat would become visible inside the newly formed cheese. Today, Morbier is still presented with a distinctive layer of ash to uphold tradition.

PROCESS: Made from raw cow milk, its maturing process lasts up to three months.

FLAVOR: Mellow and fruity flavor, fine texture.

PAIRING: Morbier tastes great with country bread dipped in white wine. It's an ideal cheese to make creamy sauces for fish dishes. Tomatoes and salads always get tastier with some cubes of Morbier. Grapes, melon, and dried fruit also pair well with it, and Chardonnay and Sauvignon wines are ideal mates for the cheese.

Le Salers

ORIGINS: Salers is said to be one of France's oldest cheeses, around 1,000 years old.

PROCESS: Wheel-shaped, known as a *meule*, and weighing between 70 and 120 pounds, Salers has a distinctive red engraved stamp bearing its first two letters, "SA." Exclusively farm-produced, its fabrication process involves strict conditions: from the specific breed of cows (Salers) to what they are fed to the container in which the cheese is prepared, the cheese-making process is really about respecting the tradition and heritage. Maturation lasts 90 days.

FLAVOR: The usual aromas are that of fruits (nuts and citrus fruits), plants (grass and hay), and lactic scents (whipped cream and butter).

PAIRING: Salers is known for pairing best with sweet foods, such as fruits (apples, grapes, cherries, or raspberries) and red wine (like Sancerre or Saumur Champigny).

Le Saint-Nectaire

ORIGINS: Dating back to the 17th century, this unctuous cheese with sweet chestnut flavor gained fame after being presented to King Louis the XIV.

PROCESS: Made in the beautiful Auvergne region, Saint-Nectaire requires a minimum of 28 days of maturation. Be aware that you may come across two types of Saint-Nectaire: farm-produced and industrial.

FLAVOR: Saint-Nectaire's aroma derives mainly from its mold. It has a smooth texture and a pronounced nutty flavor. Its crust is usually grayish, with yellow and red dots of mold.

PAIRING: Saint-Nectaire is a great cheese for tarts, pies, or even brioches.

La Tomme de Savoie

ORIGINS: Seen as the economical and cultural heritage of the Savoie region, the famous Tomme de Savoie is a generic name. In fact, there exist many variations depending on the mountains and valleys of the region where each Tomme is produced (Tomme du Mont-Cenis, Tomme de la Tarentaise, Tomme des Bauges, for example). The word *Tomme* itself refers globally to mountain cheeses.

PROCESS: Matured from June to October. When it is brought out of the cave, Tomme weighs around three-and-a-half pounds.

FLAVOR: Its pale color ranges from yellow to off-white, and its aroma is that of a cellar and mold. When it hits the tongue, Tomme develops a delicate taste of chestnut.

PAIRING: Like all cheeses, Tomme works perfectly with bread, fruits, and cured meats. Red wine from Côte-du-Rhône or white Alsace Riesling make for great flavor combinations.

Cooked, pressed cheeses
Fromages à pâte pressée cuite / À pâte dure

After pressing the curd, the cheese is heated then left to mature. It has a hard crust, a dense and firm consistency, and a smooth surface.

L'Abondance

ORIGINS: Literally meaning "abundance," this cheese got its name from the Val d'Abondance ("Abundance Valley") and the breed of Abondance cows who give their milk to make it.

PROCESS: A hundred days of maturation.

FLAVOR: Slightly bitter chestnut flavor.

PAIRING: Either served as an appetizer, in salads, or at the end of the meal.

Le Beaufort

ORIGINS: Born in the Middle Ages and named after the valley of Beaufort, this renowned cheese has been part of regional dishes for generations, such as the famous *fondue savoyarde* and the traditional *gratin de crozets*.

PROCESS: Made from the milk of Abondance or Tarine cows. After a maturation of at least five months, Beaufort weighs anywhere from 44 to 154 pounds. Shaped like a cylindrical millstone, it has a distinctive thick, concave heel.

FLAVOR: Beaufort possesses a strong odor, a firm, buttery texture, and a smooth crust with a yellow-orange color.

PAIRING: It may be served as an appetizer or on a cheese plate. Beverage-wise, it marries well with red wine. Note that this cheese isn't meant to be grated, for it will lose its taste. Rather, it's better you cut it into small cubes to put into any dish you want, like vegetables, pastas, and salads.

Le Comté

ORIGINS: Comté has a long history, dating back to the Middle Ages, making its way through centuries to become an AOC Cheese in 1958. Today it is one of the most consumed cheeses in France.

FLAVOR: Belonging to the family of Gruyère cheeses, *le Comté* has a creamy and mellow texture. It counts among the rare cheeses that prohibit artificial coloring. Comté has a grainy surface ranging from golden brown to yellow.

It's hard to name a specific flavor for Comté, as it never seems to taste the same. Experts argue that flavors vary according to places and the process and season of fabrication; even small details can affect the results. It may taste salty or sweet, acidic or bitter, fruity or spicy; it may present vegetable or fresh plant aromas, or what's referred to as "animal" aromas, like egg yolk, leather, or barn.

PAIRING: Comté pairs well with many different ingredients, even some that may be surprising, such as saffron, mango, chestnut, vanilla, fig, truffle butter, eggplant, or cherries. (Experimenting with flavors and unusual ingredients is the best way to come up with new recipes.) For wine, Comté best matches with red and white wines from the Jura region, champagne, and red or white Châteauneuf du Pape, as well as beer.

L'Emmental

ORIGINS: One of the oldest French cheeses, the Emmental from the Savoyard region is made from raw cow milk from Tarine, Abondance, or Montbéliarde breeds. Shaped like a wheel, it weighs around 165 pounds and has a diameter of 29 inches. Its crust, yellow to pale brown, has the name "Savoie" signed in red ink on the side of the round. It has distinctive round and regular holes, just like Gruyère.

FLAVOR: Mild and fruity.

PAIRING: In savory dishes, Emmental pairs well with ham, bacon, lamb, curry, turmeric, celery, red onion, and cauliflower. It also complements sweeter flavors like pear, cherry tomato, beet, fig, dried apricot, walnut, golden raisin, and fruit paste. Opt for white wine.

❊ Soft cheeses
Fromages à pâte molle

To make soft cheeses, the surface is sowed (or covered) with mold, forming a rind during maturation.

There are three different types of soft cheeses that can be distinguished by the type of rind they possess: bloomy, washed, and natural.

Soft cheeses with bloomy rinds
Fromages à pâte molle à croûte fleurie

Those soft cheeses have their rind coated with Penicillium candidum, a fungus that gives them a white color and furry texture.

Les Bries

ORIGINS: There exist around 40 types of Brie produced in France that are differentiated by region. The most well-known are Brie de Meaux, Brie de Melun, Brie de Nangis, and Brie de Provins.

PROCESS: Brie is made from raw milk and requires six to eight weeks of maturation. Its coat is white and slightly fluffy.

FLAVOR: These round, soft cheeses vary according to region and origin. Brie de Melun presents a strong smell and a fruity flavor, for instance, while Brie de Meaux has a fine flavor of chestnut. Brie de Nangis is the sweetest of all.

PAIRING: Brie can be enjoyed quite simply, as appetizers or at the end of the meal with bread and walnuts. Red wine pairs best with this cheese.

Les Briques

ORIGINS: These small rectangular cheeses (hence the name, which means "brick" in French) are made from goat milk (Brique ardéchoise, Brique rieumoise) and from cow milk (Brique du Forez).

PROCESS: To make Briques, cheese makers mix the curd with either rennet, which makes for a tender paste, or lactic culture, creating a thicker and harder paste.

FLAVOR: These Briques are famous for their tender texture and delicate flavor.

PAIRING: Ideal in salads and with white wine.

Le Camembert

ORIGINS: Few cheeses can brag about their reputation like the internationally famous Camembert, one of the most distinctive components of French culinary culture alongside baguettes and wine. Created in the 18th century, this smooth cheese originally from Normandy has the shape of a disk with a white bloomy rind.

PROCESS: Selecting cows is an important part of the cheese-making process, and Camembert is made strictly from Normandy cows. Cows have to graze for at least six months before milk can be collected to make Camembert.

FLAVOR: Earthy aroma and a strong, fruity flavor.

PAIRING: Camembert can be enjoyed spread on bread or cooked in many varied recipes, such as flaky pastries and tarts.

Les Carrés

ORIGINS: Meaning "square," according to their shape, these small cheeses come from either cow milk (Carré de Bonneville, Carré de Bray, Carré de l'Est), goat milk (Carré du Poitou), or sheep milk (Carré Corse) mixed with cream.

FLAVOR: They vary in color and taste according to the region they are made in. They usually have a tender texture and a mild but distinctive flavor.

PAIRING: Carrés may be eaten as appetizers with tomatoes or slices of bread, cooked in tarts, or enjoyed at the end of a meal with fruit.

Le Coulommiers

ORIGINS: This famous cheese from the Île-de-France region has been in existence since the Middle Ages. Today, it is one of the most-consumed cheeses in France.

PROCESS: Maturation lasts from five to eight weeks.

FLAVOR: Similar to Brie de Melun, both bitter and sweet.

PAIRING: The inside of the cheese, or the cream of Coulommiers, is used as a side to meat dishes. The cheese itself pairs best with red wine, such as Côte-du-Rhône or Bourgogne.

Le Cœur de Neufchâtel

ORIGINS: The name of this cheese comes from its heart shape (*cœur* means "heart"). It was said that during the Hundred Years' War the young women in Neufchâtel-en-Bray would offer this cheese to their lover knights.

PROCESS: Maturing lasts eight to ten weeks. The cheese is ideally consumed from April to August.

FLAVOR: While its texture and taste are similar to Camembert, the Cœur has a thicker rind and a deeper flavor.

PAIRING: Cœur is great as part of a cheese plate at the end of a meal or as a component of salads, appetizers, sauces, and desserts. You have to adapt the type of wine to pair it with according to its age: If the Cœur is young, a young, light red wine will be best. When the cheese is mature, a strong, flavorful red wine will make for a great flavor pairing.

Soft cheeses with washed rinds
Fromages à pâte molle à croûte lavée

After their surface has been washed with salt water, the rind becomes suppler, the flavors and aromas are enhanced, and the color turns red/orange.

Le Chevrotin des Aravis

ORIGINS: Another cheese born in the mountains of Savoie, the Chevrotin is made from Alpine goat milk.

PROCESS: After a maturation of three to five weeks, the Chevrotin develops a thin, pale pink rind and a tender texture.

FLAVOR: Distinctive taste of alpine flowers.

PAIRING: Goes well with red or white wine.

Le Reblochon de Savoie

ORIGINS: Created in the region of Savoie in the 13th century, Reblochon is a creamy cheese covered in thin white mold (a type of mold that reveals good maturation). When the Reblochon is farm-produced, a distinctive green patch tops the cheese.

PROCESS: Requiring a maturation of six to eight weeks, it is ideally consumed between May and October, during which the cattle enjoy the fresh rich grass of warmer days.

FLAVOR: It has an unctuous, smooth texture and fine, nutty flavor.

PAIRING: Reblochon is great as an appetizer with vegetables and herbs, on slices of bread, in a dish with potatoes, or in a tart.

Le Livarot

ORIGINS: Livarot from Normandy dates back to the 17th century. Also known as *le colonel* ("the colonel") it is recognized by its orange rind and the reed maces wrapped around its body.

PROCESS: Aging lasts six to eight weeks. It is usually enjoyed from May to September.

FLAVOR: Strong odor. Livarot's flavor varies from very pronounced to almost nonexistent when very ripe.

PAIRING: A strong red wine will pair best with this cheese, such as Saint-Julien or Pomerol.

Le Munster

ORIGINS: Dating back to the 9th century, Munster comes from the noun *monastère* ("monastery"), and it best represents the region of Alsace, where it is produced, and its soil.

PROCESS: At least 21 days are required for Munster to mature.

FLAVOR: While its texture is supple and soft, its odor and flavor are quite strong and reminiscent of the pastures on which the cows graze.

PAIRING: Munster is usually used for the regional dish *raclette* of Savoie, which consists of different types of cheeses melted in one cooking pot and eaten with bread. In Alsace, it is consumed with hot potatoes instead of bread, while in Haute-Alsace it is enjoyed with salads.

Le Maroilles

ORIGINS: In the Middle Ages, this cheese was referred to as "the marvelous Maroilles." The Maroilles hasn't lost its sparkle since to this day it is still the most popular cheese consumed in northern France.

PROCESS: Only milk from cows of the Prim'Holstein breed is used to make the famous Maroilles. Ripening lasts five to seven weeks.

FLAVOR: Shaped like a square with a pale orange coating, Maroilles possesses a distinctive and flavorful aroma.

PAIRING: Maroilles is used for tarts, on cheese plates, or as a side for dishes such as filet mignon or roasted rabbit. Champagne, or white wine such as Gewurztraminer, will pair ideally with Maroilles.

Le Pont-l'Évêque

ORIGINS: This cheese from the town of Pont-l'Évêque in Normandy is one of the most popular cheeses in France today and among the oldest, dating back to the 12th century.

PROCESS: Aging lasts two weeks. The cheese can be consumed all year, as a constant mild and humid climate makes for good grass for cows.

FLAVOR: Its soft texture, glossy rind, developed odor, and nutty, fruity aromas make it a hearty cheese.

PAIRING: Dried fruits, hazelnuts, and a flavorful red wine such as Pomerol, Volnay, or Bourgueil are perfect pairs for this cheese.

Soft cheeses with natural rinds
Fromages à pâte molle à croûte naturelle

Soft cheeses with natural rinds are mainly produced from goat milk. Compared to other cheeses, they have no mold inside or outside, while their rind forms spontaneously and is not washed during maturation.

Le Chabichou du Poitou

ORIGINS: Shaped like a small cylinder, the Chabichou, born in the 19th century, sounds as cute to say as it is good to eat.

PROCESS: Raw or pasteurized goat milk solely from Poitou region goats is used. Maturation lasts two to three weeks.

FLAVOR: When fresh, this cheese has a moist and supple texture with a distinct mild goat cheese flavor. When dry, its rind is strong and its taste much more pronounced.

PAIRING: Chabichou works well as an appetizer. The Chabichou should be enjoyed with wine from the same region, such as Sauvignon Blanc or the light red wine des Deux-Sèvres.

Le Crottin de Chavignol

ORIGINS: Created in the 18th century, Crottin de Chavignol got its name from the ancient word *crot*, meaning "hole."

PROCESS: Crottin de Chavignol is quite quick to make and be enjoyed, requiring only 10 days of maturation. Depending on the degree of maturation, texture and flavor will vary.

FLAVOR: Age affects the color and taste of the Crottin: When of medium age (five days), it has a goat milk flavor. When mature and old (ten days), it has a bluish aspect and a pleasant nutty flavor.

PAIRING: Great as an appetizer and at the end of a meal, Crottin is also used in recipes such as *tourte au Chavignol* (a thick, round tart), *Chavignol sur canapé de pommes* (a Crottin and apple sandwich heated in the oven), the *croque-madame au Chavignol* (a ham and egg sandwich) or in *salade de chèvre chaud* (warmed Crottin in salad). It matches well with white wines such as Sancerre, Pouilly Fumé, or Quincy.

Le Rocamadour

ORIGINS: Born in the southwest of France, Rocamandour has been around since the 15th century.

PROCESS: Maturation must last a minimum of 12 to 15 days.

FLAVOR: Bright flavor of hazelnut.

PAIRING: This creamy, unctuous cheese is a delight to eat before, during, or after meals. It can be enjoyed alone, on toast, in salads, on a cheese plate, or in a tart with vegetables.

ORIGINS OF THE NAME CROTTIN
LES ORIGINES DU NOM CROTTIN

Crottin itself literally means "dung"—quite a surprising name for a cheese, you might think. *Crottin* is a generic name that can refer to certain types of goat cheeses. Legend has it that the name came from the fact that when cheeses were first being made, some of them would dry and turn brown during maturation. Thankfully, cheese *crottins* taste nothing like *crottin* itself.

Le Pélardon

ORIGINS: First made in the Languedoc region in southern France in the 18th century, the name Pélardon comes from the Cévenol dialect word *pébre*, meaning "pepper".

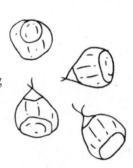

PROCESS: Maturing for at least three weeks, Pélardon is ideally consumed from May to September.

FLAVOR: Light spicy flavor with a strong nutty note.

PAIRING: This small, round goat cheese with a firm texture is delicious as a starter. It may be cooked in breadcrumbs and enjoyed with a little olive oil. Pélardon can also be found on cheese plates. In the Cévennes region, it is served with blueberries or heather honey.

Le Valençay

ORIGINS: Valençay is uniquely shaped like a truncated pyramid. Some attribute its shape to the Prince de Talleyrand under Napoleon's empire. Napoleon had just come back from a disastrous campaign in Egypt, and when the prince saw these pyramid-shaped cheeses, he ordered them to be truncated so that the emperor wouldn't be reminded of his failure in Egypt. Others claim that the cheese is actually shaped after the church bell of Levroux (in the center of France).

PROCESS: Eleven days minimum of maturation are required.

FLAVOR: With its pale blue and gray color and tender crust, the Valençay tastes slightly like fresh walnuts or dried fruits.

PAIRING: Valençay pairs well with any type of wine from the same region, red, rosé, or white. It may be enjoyed in entrées, as a snack, or at the end of the meal.

Fresh curd cheeses *Fromages à pâte fraîche*

Fresh curd cheeses haven't been matured or fermented. The milk is warmed slightly, coagulated with rennet and then placed in the fridge. They don't have a rind, their color is white, their texture is mellow, and they possess a fresh, light, and pleasant aroma.

PROCESSED CHEESES
FROMAGES À PÂTE FONDUE

Processed cheeses are typically made from normal cheese with added emulsifiers and various unfermented dairy ingredients. They are found in supermarkets rather than in cheese shops. Most cheese aficionados are repelled by such industrialized and commercial cheeses, whose fabrication is far from artisanal and whose taste is way below that of a Cantal or a Comté.

Some of the most common and popular processed cheeses are:

- La Cancoillotte, which has an unctuous, runny texture and salty, sharp flavor. (You can also find an artisanal version, although the commercial cheese is more common.)

- Le Fort de Béthune, which has a has a very strong odor and flavor; to those unfamiliar with it, it may even stink.

- Le Kiri, a popular cheese among children, is made from mostly *fromage blanc*, and has a smooth, spreadable consistency with a very light and salty flavor. (This cheese can also be found as a farm-made cheese.)

- La Vache qui Rit—You may already be familiar with the Laughing Cow—the famous happy red cow with its single earring. There isn't much of a difference from Kiri: It has a mellow, creamy texture and a salty taste.

La Caillebotte

ORIGINS: Born in the west region of the Poitou-Charente in the 15th century, the Caillebotte is made from cow milk.

FLAVOR: Smooth, mellow texture and sweet, fruity flavor.

PAIRING: Caillebotte is usually consumed in summer because of its refreshing taste. It may be used as a substitute for whipped cream, a side for fruit salads, or flavored with coffee extract or cinnamon and eaten as dessert.

Le fromage blanc

ORIGINS: The most famous of fresh curd cheeses, the *fromage blanc* ("white cheese") is found in most kitchens in France.

FLAVOR: Smooth, creamy texture with a sweet and slightly acidic taste.

PAIRING: It may be eaten at breakfast, with cereal (instead of milk) or with fruits such as red berries, apples, and pears; as a starter, along with herbs, shallots, and spinach; within dishes like tarts, salad dressing, omelets, or sandwiches; and as dessert, with sugar, jam, or honey.

❊ Blue-veined cheeses
Fromages à pâte persillée

Blue-veined cheeses have their curd sowed and pierced so that mushrooms can form throughout the cheese. Penicillum is mixed with the milk, which is responsible for the predominant blue colors in the cheese. They develop colors ranging from blue to green to gray, hence their name. They are made from cow and sheep milk.

Le Bleu

ORIGINS: *Bleu* is a generic name referring to many types of blue-veined cheeses.

FLAVOR: Flavors differ according to the types of *bleu*: you may try the Bleu de Bresse (slightly pronounced taste, odor of mold), Bleu de Gex (supple crust with a slightly bitter taste), Bleu de Laqueuille (fresh, penetrating odor with pronounced flavor), Bleu d'Auvergne (pronounced taste although not excessive, slightly supple texture), or Bleu des Causses (melting texture, sharp flavor, pleasant smell).

PAIRING: These small Roquefort lookalikes, due to their blueish, grayish mold, are great in salads, on pizza, on cheese plates, or served with white wine.

Le Roquefort

ORIGINS: Born in the 11th century, Roquefort went on to become one of the most internationally known French cheeses. A symbol of French agricultural excellence and gastronomy, it has a distinctive look and smell that sets it apart from other cheeses.

PROCESS: Roquefort is made from sheep milk and goes through a maturation process of at least three to five months.

FLAVOR: You may know that Roquefort smells and tastes quite bitter and strong, so much that the French sometimes use the name "Roquefort" to refer to someone or something that stinks (which is quite unkind to this delicious cheese).

PAIRING: Its ivory color is sprinkled with blue-, gray-, or green-colored mold. With its strong taste, it is used in many recipes such as tarts, quiches, *feuilletés* (flaky pastries), omelets, pies, and, of course, on cheese plates. It goes great with Port or a sweet white wine like Sauternes.

✺ Inquiring
Demander

What kinds of Brie do you have?
Quels types de Brie avez-vous?

Do you have Rocamandour?
Vous auriez du Rocamandour?

Was animal or vegetable rennet used in making your cheese?
Est-ce de la presure animale ou végétale qui a été utilisée pour la fabrication des fromages?

Are your eggs from free-range hens?
Vos œufs proviennent-ils de poules élevées en plein air?

What cheese combines best with Beaujolais wine?
Quel fromage se marierait le mieux avec un Beaujolais?

Can you choose a few of your favorite cheeses for me?
Pouvez-vous me sélectionner quelques uns de vos fromages?

❊ Ordering
Commander

I would like...
Je souhaiterais...

> a crottin de chèvre, please.
> *un crottin de chèvre, s'il vous plaît.*

> to buy the strongest-flavored cheese you have.
> *acheter votre fromage le plus corsé.*

> to prepare a cheese plate for dinner. What do you suggest?
> *préparer un plateau fromage pour un dîner. Que me conseillez-vous?*

I'll have...
Je vais prendre...

> this small Brie.
> *ce petit Brie.*

> a slice of that delicious-looking Emmental.
> *une part de cet Emmental qui a l'air excellent.*

> some of the same Beaufort as yesterday.
> *un peu du même Beaufort qu'hier.*

Can I have a taste of the Roquefort you have?
Pourrais-je goûter un morceau du Roquefort que vous avez?

Can I have half of a Reblochon, please?
Pourrais-je avoir la moitié d'un Reblochon, s'il vous plaît?

TIPS ON ORDERING AT THE CHEESE SHOP
CONSEILS POUR ACHETER DU FROMAGE À UNE FROMAGERIE

If you are uncertain on the quantity of cheese you should order—let's say, to prepare a certain dish—don't hesitate to ask the *fromager*. They'll be happy to inform you and provide you with the right amount.

At a cheese shop, you'll most usually order cheeses individually, or if they are larger, a piece of the desired cheese (*un morceau* or *une part*). The seller will determine with you how large you want it.

Cheese makers are passionate about their products, so let them guide and surprise you!

Chapter 9

AT THE PRODUCE STORE

Chez le primeur

Le primeur not only sells fruits and vegetables, but also dried fruit, nuts, herbs, and spices. Here are some basic words you'll find useful.

Bitter
Amer

Dry / Dried
Sec / Séché

Firm
Ferme

Fresh
Frais

Juicy
Juteux

Ripe
Mûr

Rotten
Pourri

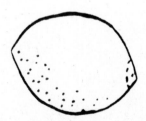

Soft
Mou

※ Fruits
Les fruits

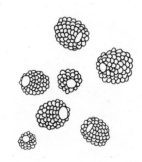

Apple
La pomme

Apricot
L'abricot

Avocado
L'avocat

Banana
La banane

Bergamot orange
La bergamote

Blackberry
La mûre

Blackcurrant
Le cassis

Blueberry
La myrtille

Cantaloupe
Le melon

Cherry
La cerise

Mirabelle (small yellow) plum
La mirabelle

Clementine
La clémentine

Currant
La groseille

Damson plum
La quetsche

Fig (fresh or dried)
La figue (fraîche ou séchée)

Grapefruit
Le pamplemousse

Grape
Le raisin

Kiwi
Le kiwi

Lemon
Le citron

Mandarin orange
La mandarine

Nectarine
La nectarine

Orange
L'orange

Peach
La pêche

Pear
La poire

Pineapple
L'ananas

Plum
La prune

Quince
Le coing

Rasberry
La framboise

Strawberry
La fraise

Watermelon
La pastèque

BERRIES
LES FRUITS ROUGES

Although "berry" is translated as *baie* in French, people don't usually use it. Instead, they refer to *fruits rouges* ("red berries"), which includes red and dark berries such as strawberries, raspberries, cherries, blueberries, blackberries, and black currants.

❋Vegetables
Les légumes

Artichoke / Artichoke heart
L'artichaut / Le cœur d'artichaut

Arugula
La roquette

Aspargus
L'asperge

Bean sprouts
Les germes de soja

Beet
La betterave

Beet greens
Les fanes de betterave

Bell pepper (green bell pepper, red bell pepper...)
Le poivron (le poivron vert, le poivron rouge...)

Broccoli
Le brocoli

Brussels sprouts
Les choux de Bruxelles

Cabbage
Le chou

Carrot
La carotte

Cauliflower
Le chou-fleur

Celery
Le céleri

Chard
La blette

Cucumber
Le concombre

Dandelion greens
Le pissenlit
Can be used in salads, soups, sandwiches, or paired with goat cheese.

Fennel
Le fenouil

Frisée
La frisée

Eggplant
L'aubergine

Endive
L'endive

Green bean
Le haricot vert

Kale
Le chou frisé

Mâche (lamb's lettuce)
La mâche

Leek
Le poireau

Lettuce
La laitue

Onion
L'oignon

Pea
Le petit-pois

Potato
La pomme de terre

Pumpkin
La citrouille / Le potiron

Radish
Le radis

Salad greens
La salade

Shallot
L'échalote

Spinach
Les épinards

Tomato / A bunch of tomatoes
La tomate / Une grappe de tomates

Turnip
Le navet

Winter squash
La courge

Zucchini
La courgette

✻ Herbs, spices, and seasonings
Herbes, épices, et assaisonnements

Basil
Le basilic

Black pepper
Le poivre noir

Capers
Des câpres

Chervil
Le cerfeuil

Chive
La ciboulette

Clove
Le clou de girofle

Coriander
La coriandre

Fines herbs
Les fines herbes

A combination of herbs typical to French cuisine, used to garnish a dish, consisting of parsley, tarragon, chives, and chervil. You can buy and make your own fresh fines herbes mix, or purchase it in supermarkets dried in small bottles.

Garlic / A clove of garlic
L'ail / Une gousse d'ail

Ginger
Le gingembre

Mint
La menthe

Nutmeg
La noix de muscade

Oregano
L'origan

Parsley (flat-leaf / curly-leaf)
Le persil (persil plat / persil frisé)

Rosemary
Le romarin

Saffron
Le safran

Shallot
L'échalote

Tarragon
L'estragon

Thyme
Le thym

❋ Condiments
Les condiments

Olive
L'olive

Olive oil
L'huile d'olive

Mustard
La moutarde

Mayonnaise
La mayonnaise

Pickle
Le cornichon

Vinegar
Le vinaigre

Balsamic vinegar
Le vinaigre balsamique

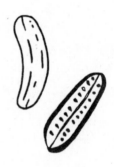

❋ Nuts and dried fruits
Les noix et les fruits secs

Almond
L'amande

Chestnut
La châtaigne / Le marron

Hazelnut
La noisette

Peanut
La cacahuète

Pine nut
Le pignon de pin

Pistachio
La pistache

Walnut
La noix

Dried apricot
L'abricot sec

Dried banana
La banane séchée

Date
La datte

Dried fig
La figue séchée

Raisin
Le raisin sec

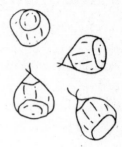

❊ Inquiring
Demander

Primeurs all work differently. Unlike at the farmers' market, most of them will let you pick and choose produce at your own convenience; others will select your fruits and vegetables for you.

I'd like...
J'aimerais...

> **two baskets of strawberries.**
> *deux barquettes de fraises.*
>
> **a ripe peach.**
> *une pêche mûre.*
>
> **a bunch of mint, basil, and parsley**
> *une botte de menthe, de basilic et de persil.*

Can I get...
Puis-je avoir...

> **one cluster of firm tomatoes?**
> *une grappe de tomates bien fermes?*
>
> **a handful of walnuts?**
> *une poignée de noix?*
>
> **two pounds of potatoes?**
> *un kilo de pommes de terres?*

❊ Eating organic
Manger bio

Organic food is slowly but steadily making its way into shops and carts. The French are beginning to understand the importance of buying food free of pesticides, preservatives, and chemicals. Farmers themselves are engaging in healthier methods of production and cultivation, more organic shops are opening in cities, and organic farmers' markets are expanding.

If you're aiming to buy organic products in supermarkets, look for the most famous brand of organic products: Bjorg. From soy milk to cookies to quinoa, Bjorg is the first name in organics, and it is distributed in most shops. Naturalia is the equivalent of Whole Foods in France, although it's much, much smaller in size! Almost all supermarkets, such as Monoprix or Carrefour, sell their own lines of organic products as well. You just need to look for the official green label "AB" (*Agriculture Biologique*, meaning "Organic Agriculture").

Is this / Are these...
Est-ce que c'est... / Est-ce qu'ils sont...

> **organic?**
> *bio?*
>
> **healthy?**
> *sain(s)?*

pesticide-free?
sans pesticides?

locally grown?
cultivé(s) localement?

I...
Je...

believe in eating healthy.
suis pour manger sain.

only buy organic products.
n'achète que des produits bios.

You...
Tu...

should start eating healthy.
devrais commencer à manger sain.

should go see this entirely organic farmers' market.
devrais aller voir ce marché entièrement bio.

Do you grow your own vegetables?
Cultivez-vous vos propres légumes?

Do you make your own cheese?
Faites-vous votre propre fromage?

SECTION III

BEVERAGES

Boissons

There's one thing the French enjoy as much as a good meal: a good drink. Whether it be a glass of rosé during a family summer lunch, a cold beer with colleagues or friends after work at the local pub, a fruity red wine on a fancy dinner date, or a vigorous shot of vodka on a Saturday night out on the town, a drink can be enjoyed on any occasion, on one condition: that it is shared.

Shared drinks, just like shared meals, not only ease communication, bring people together, and create new friendships—but they definitely taste better when you're together. (Just make sure you're sharing a drink with someone older than 18, the legal age to buy alcohol in France.)

Chapter 10

WINE

Le vin

To talk about French *boissons* (beverages), one must begin with the most famous one: wine.

In France, drinking wine is so natural no one questions it. The rare souls who don't drink wine—or worse, who have *never* drunk wine—are stared at like they're strange creatures.

A meal is never as good as when it is paired with a glass of wine, which enhances flavors and enchants the senses. During family lunches or dinners at friends' houses, one or two bottles of wine are always present on the table (offering a bottle of wine when you're invited to someone's home is the most natural and appreciated gift). Wine is deeply embedded in culture and habits, and it is synonymous with conviviality.

All generations and all social classes enjoy wine. A bottle can be bought anywhere, from a convenience store to a supermarket to a wine shop. It can be extremely expensive (some bottles can cost up to thousands of euros) and affordable as well—you can find bottles in supermarkets as cheap as three euros!

France is the world's leading wine producer, ahead of Italy and Spain, with an astounding 502 million cases of wine produced (12 bottles per box). Wine, like cheese, is divided into many families according to the regions where it is produced and the soil where the vines are cultivated. Just like cheese, it will taste differently depending on its age and which type of dish you pair it with. Wine is also generally named by the geographic area it comes from.

To get to know French wine better, here is some necessary vocabulary.

Red wine
Le vin rouge

White wine
Le vin blanc

Rosé wine
Le vin rosé

Sparkling wine
Le vin mousseux / Le vin pétillant / Le crément

Champagne
Le champagne

A glass of red wine
Un verre de rouge

A glass of white wine
Un verre de blanc

A glass of rosé
Un verre de rosé

Wine glass
Un verre à vin

Champagne flute
Une flûte à champagne

Glass of champagne
Une coupe (de champagne)

A bottle of wine
Une bouteille de vin

A bottle of champagne
Une bouteille de champagne

A half-bottle
Une demi-bouteille

A (wine) jug
Un pichet (de vin)

A carafe of wine
Une carafe de vin

Come on, let's have a glass of champagne!
Allez, on se prend une coupe!

Could you put this bottle in a wine bucket with ice?
Pourriez-vous mettre cette bouteille dans un seau à vin avec des glaçons?

FRENCH WINE REGIONS

CHAMPAGNE

Paris

Strasbourg

ALSACE

LOIRE

BOURGOGNE

JURA

BEAUJOLAIS

SAVOIE

BORDEAUX

SUD-OUEST

VALLEE
DU RHONE

Biarritz

PROVENCE COTE D'AZUR

Marseille

LANGUEDOC ROUSSILLON

❀ The art of wine
L'art du vin

When you look at a map of France, it is easy to see just how varied the geography of the country is. From the snow-capped Alps to the Mediterranean, from the untamed Atlantic coast to austere land-locked Champagne, it is clear that location determines how the French eat. But the same is obviously true for how they produce the wine they drink.

Le terroir

Terroir refers to all of the factors (sunshine, wind, soil, rain) of a specific patch of land that give a wine its unique personality. But it's also the embodiment of the winemaker's craft, knowledge, and intuition. Unlike many New World wines that try to reproduce the same standard taste from different countries around the globe, in France, winemakers embrace the differences and individuality that *terroir* gives a wine. *Terroir* is rigorously scientific and literally down-to-earth but also nebulous and emotional, making it a concept that is quintessentially French.

You can feel the terroir of this wine; it's just like being in Provence!

Tu peux sentir le terroir de ce vin; on se croirait en Provence!

Appellation

Appellation refers to the strict geographical location where a particular wine is produced. French law codifies exact locations where grapes are grown, the varieties of grapes used, and every step of production, including how and where a wine is bottled and aged. If these stringent conditions are met for that particular *appellation*, a wine earns the right to put the prized letters *AOC* (*Appellation d'origine contrôlée*) on its label. Even if you are drinking a sparkling wine from Burgundy (next door to Champagne country), made from the same grapes grown on the same type of limestone soil and produced with the same methods that they use in the Champagne region, you are *not* drinking champagne. Remember: in France, the word champagne is *not* synonymous with just any fizzy wine. Wines that don't meet the charter for a particular AOC are sold under a variety of labels including *vin de table* (table wine) and *vin de pays* (country wine). Some of these wines can be pleasant surprises. But beware, the opposite is true as well: Having an AOC doesn't automatically mean that you'll be drinking a fine wine.

Cépage

When you order a glass of Pinot Noir or Sauvignon Blanc, you are referring to a *cépage*, the variety of grape that went into making the wine. But in France, the place where it was made is just as important as the grape itself. If you want to show off your wine savviness, try ordering wine by its origin, not its grape. You can always casually drop your knowledge of its *cépage* into your conversation later.

> **Try this Marsannay. It's made with Pinot Beurot, not the Chardonnay you usually find in Burgundy.**
> *Essaie ce Marsannay. C'est du Pinot Beurot, non du Chardonnay qu'on trouve en Bourgogne d'habitude.*

Choosing a wine
Choisir un vin

Red or white? Still or sparkling? Budget or break-the-bank? If you don't know where to begin, think about when and where you're drinking. If you're having summer salad on the patio of a *mas* (traditional country house) in Provence, a locally produced Bandol rosé, crisp and chilled, might be exactly what you're looking for. With a platter of oysters, try a Loire region Muscadet. Or whatever you're celebrating, from a romantic dinner to a reunion of family and friends, popping open a bottle of champagne never fails to make an occasion special. If you are still not sure what you want, look locally. While you're traveling through France, ask about wines from the region. There is a good chance that local wine will complement local food. And never hesitate to ask for advice. Formal restaurants will have *sommeliers,* trained wine stewards, who will guide you through sometimes daunting wine lists, but even at your neighborhood *bistrot*, the waiter or owner will always be happy to help. Tell them what you're eating, what you like, and possibly how much you want to spend, and they will do the rest.

Can you suggest a wine from the area for us?
Pourriez-vous nous conseiller un vin de la région?

I don't know what to order. I'll let you choose!
Je ne sais pas quoi commander. Je vous laisse le choix!

SIMPLE GUIDELINES FOR WINE PAIRINGS
PETIT GUIDE DES ACCORDS ENTRE PLATS ET VINS

There are exceptions to each of these rules, but if you're wondering where to start, these are some very basic wine pairings you need to know:

- Red wine is great with red meat, duck, game, and a wide range of flavorful cheeses.
- Dry white wine is meant for white meat, fish, and seafood. Sweet white wines can be served with dessert, but are also great over a foie gras or even a Roquefort cheese.
- Rosé pairs best with light meals, such as salads and cold meats.
- For dishes cooked with wine, whenever possible drink the wine that went into the sauce.

Just to get you started, here are a few wines to consider. The list is not exhaustive, and remember, within a given region, or even within the same winery, quality and price can vary greatly. There is only one way to know: Try more and more wines (in moderation, of course!).

Cheap chic
Chic et pas cher

Contrary to popular belief, you don't need to max out your credit cards to get a great bottle of wine. For under the €10-mark (about $13) and often even under €5, you can find wines that represent great value and great drinking. In restaurants, expect 50–100% markups.

Muscadet

Several *appellations* from the west of the Loire Valley up to the limits of the city of Nantes fall under this heading. The label of this white wine sometimes says that it is *sur lie*, meaning the wine has been left in contact with the yeast deposits that naturally form during fermentation, developing its bright taste.

REGION: Loire

CÉPAGES: Melon blanc

NOTES: fruity, fresh, crisp

READY TO DRINK: after a year or two

KEEP: generally no more than five years

PAIRINGS: raw oysters, seafood platters, fish dishes

Riesling

One of the most popular whites from Alsace, its roots can be traced back to the 9th century.

REGION: Alsace

CÉPAGE: Riesling

NOTES: green, floral, mineral

READY TO DRINK: at two years

KEEP: up to ten years

PAIRINGS: local *choucroute garnie* (preserved cabbage cooked with sausages and cured meats), but also dishes with a touch of spice

Saint-Chinian

These wines are made in the *arrière-pays* of the slopes of the Hérault, the countryside a few miles inland from the Mediterranean coast outside of the town of Béziers. The production is mostly red.

REGION: Languedoc-Roussillon

CÉPAGES: often a blend including Syrah, Grenache, Mourvèdre, and Carignan, among others.

NOTES: powerful (sometimes packing a serious alcoholic punch), red fruits, minerals, spice, earth

READY TO DRINK: young

KEEP: no more than five years

PAIRINGS: cured meats or a rack of lamb roasted with *herbes de Provence*

Bergerac or Côtes-de-Bergerac

Like the region of southwest France where they come from, the red wines of Bergerac are hearty, generous, and easy to drink with a variety of foods.

REGION: Sud-Ouest

CÉPAGES: Merlot, Cabernet-Sauvignon, Cabernet Franc

NOTES: heady, snappy, aromatics, berries

READY TO DRINK: after one or two years

KEEP: five or more years

PAIRINGS: *cassoulet* (a stew of white bean and meats), *grillons* (a spreadable pâté made of pork, duck, or goose)

Sure bets
Valeurs sûres

If you're looking for a versatile wine for a dinner party, a family meal, or a candlelit dinner, every region produces excellent wines that will suit your needs. Here are some of the *appellations* that will garner nods of approval from your fellow diners. On average, you'll spend between €10–25 in a wine shop, and often a bit more for wines from the most reputable cellars.

Sancerre

While this section of the Loire produces solid reds and rosés, the stars of the *appellation* are still the whites. This is a classic choice for seafood, mild dishes, and some cheeses.

REGION: Loire

CÉPAGE: Sauvignon Blanc

NOTES: mineral, grass, citrus, flowers

READY TO DRINK: at one year

KEEP: five years, sometimes more

PAIRINGS: seafood, *saumon à l'oseille* (salmon in sorrel sauce), soft cheeses like Camembert and drier cheeses like *crottin de chavignol* (a goat cheese that comes from the same area)

Chablis

Chablis is a consistently reliable white from Burgundy that reflects a wide variety of styles, in part due to the winemaker's choice to use oak barrels or not for aging their wine. The use of wood and the amount of time the wine stays in the barrels in the process are key elements to each vineyard's "recipe." Look for Petit Chablis and Chablis Grand Cru for something even more special.

REGION: Burgundy

CÉPAGE: Chardonnay (or its local name, *beaunois*)

NOTES: depending on the wine, you might recognize wild mushroom, butter, brioche, or minerals

READY TO DRINK: within one to three years

KEEP: some will keep ten years or more

PAIRINGS: broiled scallops or grilled tuna with Chablis aged in oak barrels, *blanquette de veau* and other creamy, mild dishes with un-oaked wines

Châteauneuf-du-Pape

In the 14th century, the popes relocated from Rome to the southern French town of Avignon. They didn't stay, but their heritage in the area includes the opulent Papal Palace in Avignon and the wineries a few miles outside the fortified walls in the Rhône valley. Don't miss the excellent whites from this *appellation* as well.

REGION: Côtes-du-Rhône

CÉPAGES: (reds) Grenache Noir, Syrah, Mourvèdre, Cinsault among many others

NOTES: red cherries, black currants, blackberries, roasted coffee

READY TO DRINK: wait at least two or three years, often more

KEEP: up to 10, 15, or 20 years and in some exceptional cases many more

PAIRINGS: strong-flavored meats like wild game, grilled kidneys, sautéed wild mushrooms, ratatouille

Extraordinary wines
Vins d'exception

These are indeed extraordinary wines that involve more than just financial investment. A wine cellar is needed to ensure that these wines are kept in optimal conditions (along with a couple of decades of patience). The cost easily rises to the hundreds or even thousands for a single bottle.

Château Petrus

A Pomerol, but not just one of your run-of-the-mill Bordeaux, Petrus is one of the names that people whisper with respect. The price of a bottle that can easily hit the thousands might have something to do with the awe the wine inspires, or due to the careful harvesting (just after the morning dew has evaporated but before the sun gets too hot), too. A more modest, but by no means cheap, alternative would be a Haut-Médoc *Grand Cru Classé*.

REGION: Bordeaux

CÉPAGES: Merlot with some Cabernet Franc thrown in

NOTES: cedar, tobacco, licorice, truffle, ripe berries

READY TO DRINK: sooner than other grand wines; it might be ready to drink after seven to ten years

KEEP: 50-plus years under the right conditions

PAIRINGS: *filet de bœuf sauce marchand de vin*, also called *à la bordelaise* (beef tenderloin in a red wine reduction)

Romanée-Conti

Only about 6,000 bottles of the grandest of the great Burgundies is produced every year. Years of careful aging are needed for this ruby wine to release its dizzying bouquet. As of this writing, 1992 should be just about ready to drink, though it probably won't peak for a few years yet. If the price tag makes your eyes water, look nearby, maybe a Vosne-Romanée Premier Cru. For a noble white, you could try a Chassagne-Montrachet that grows next to Romanée-Conti.

REGION: Burgundy

CÉPAGE: Pinot Noir

NOTES: heady, ripe plums, rose petals

READY TO DRINK: don't even think about opening that bottle in the first two decades

KEEP: half a century or more

PAIRINGS: roast pheasant, *truffes sous la cendre* (whole truffles roasted in the glowing embers of a wood fire), *chapon rôti aux cèpes* (porcini-stuffed capon—a rooster that has been castrated to make its flesh more succulent)

Château d'Yquem

This Sauternes is one of the mythical wines of Bordeaux. The *pourriture noble* ("noble rot," or fine mold that the grapes develop in the high humidity of the region) are at the root of the complex flavors. If the producers decide that a year's production isn't up to par, they simply don't make the wine and sell it off under another label. If you're looking for a sweet white wine that is much friendlier to your wallet, you could try other Sauternes like a Barsac. For a real bargain, try a Saussignac from the Southwest.

REGION: Bordeaux

CÉPAGES: sémillon, Sauvignon Blanc

NOTES: sweet but not cloying; hazelnut, burnt orange, honey

READY TO DRINK: about 20 years

KEEP: a century or more

PAIRINGS: *pigeon farci au foie gras* (roast squab stuffed with foie gras)

WINES YOU MAY HAVE NEVER HEARD OF
DES VINS DONT VOUS N'AVEZ PEUT-ÊTRE PAS ENTENDU PARLER

One of the joys of traveling around France is finding local wines that you might not find readily elsewhere. Try tannic reds like Pécharmant with the hearty foods of the southwest; thin Arbois and Mondeuse pair with a cheese fondue in the Alps; distinctive *vins de paille* (the grapes are dried on straw mats before being fermented) are made in several regions of France; and *cépages* that are unique to the island of Corsica like the niellucciu grape. Even in regions that are familiar for their big-name wines, there are countless smaller *appellations* just waiting to be discovered, like Fixin or Bouzeron in Burgundy.

Champagnes and sparkling wines
Champagnes et vins pétillants

Contrary to popular belief, for champagne, all the aging happens in the winemaker's cellar. Once it's been bottled, it is ready to drink and shouldn't be kept more than a couple of years, three or four at most. Keep a bottle of bubbly in the fridge for those unplanned celebrations, but just make sure you have something to celebrate and refresh your stock on a regular basis. Here is a little champagne guide *(un petit guide du champagne)*

Brut vs. demi-sec

Brut champagnes are dry, *demi-sec* (literally, "half-dry") champagnes are sweet; just to keep you on your toes, however, "*extra dry*" is sweeter than *brut*.

Cépages

The *cépages* that go into champagne are Pinot Noir, Pinot Meunier, and Chardonnay.

Consistent flavor

Most champagne is non-vintage, meaning the winemaker's art is finding the perfect balance to produce the same wine, year in and year out. This is done by mixing various wines from different combinations of grapes fermented to different degrees. Every few years, individual houses decide that they have the makings of a *millésimé* (a distinctive vintage). These are sometimes also labeled *cuvée spéciale* or "special blend."

Which house?

Among the most prestigious names in champagne, you'll find Dom Pérignon and Krug. Ruinart, Pol Roger, and Nicolas Feuillatte may not be the biggest names, but their wines are available around the globe. And of course, seek out the little producers in the region whose bottles don't make it to the big wine shops or restaurants. To learn more about the history and production of the jewel of French wines, go on cellar tours while you are there. All tours will include a tasting of the house's champagnes.

Alternatives

If you don't want to splash out on champagne, more affordable alternatives include *crémants* (*de Bourgogne, de Loire, d'Alsace* are a few examples). Sparkling wines from every region more than hold their own compared to their noble cousins. Try sparkling wines from Vouvray in the Loire Valley, Saint-Péray in the Côtes-du-Rhône, or a Gaillac from the southwest. *Vin pétillant, vin mousseux,* and (in the case of Gaillac) *perlé* are other terms that identify sparkling wines.

A CHEATER'S GUIDE TO WINE
L'ANTI-SÈCHE DU VIN

Who says you can't judge a book by its cover? There are no hard and fast rules with 100% guarantees, but even if you don't know the first thing about a wine, you can learn a lot from a bottle just by looking it.

- Is the glass thick and dark? If so, it means that the producer spent a little more on a better bottle because it is a better wine that deserves to be protected by good glass.
- Does the base of the bottle have an indentation thick enough to put your thumb in? The indentation creates a ridge where deposits will naturally form as the wine ages, again suggesting that the producer feels the wine will improve over time.
- Conversely, if the glass is light and the bottom flat, it's

a wine that is meant to be drunk young, as in right now.

- Look at the foil over the cork. If it says "Récoltant," it means that the producer who grew the wine made the wine, increasing the chances that they cared about preserving the *terroir*.

- If you have to choose between two wines you know nothing about with similar *appellations*, say Beaujolais and Beaujolais Villages, or Bergerac or Côtes-de-Bergerac, go for the more specific *Villages* or the *Côtes*. The terms often designate the more exclusive part of an *appellation*. The usage is a little different, but the same idea applies to wines that append the terms *grand cru* or *premier cru*.

❧ Ordering and purchasing wine
Commander et acheter du vin

May I...
Puis-je...

> **have a glass of red wine?**
> *avoir un verre de rouge?*

> **taste your Chinon?**
> *goûter votre Chinon?*

> **see your wine menu?**
> *voir votre carte des vins?*

Is there a cellar tour in English today?
Y a-t-il une visite des caves en anglais aujourd'hui?

Can we have a tasting?
Peut-on faire une dégustation?

I would like...
J'aimerais...

> **to try the Gewurztraminer. I've never tasted it before.**
> *essayer le Gewurztraminer. Je n'en ai jamais goûté avant.*

> **a second glass of rosé, please.**
> *un deuxième verre de rosé, s'il vous plaît.*

> **you to taste the Sancerre. It's one of the best wines.**
> *que tu goûtes le Sancerre. C'est un des meilleurs vins.*

> **a glass of white wine instead of red.**
> *un verre de blanc au lieu d'un rouge.*

Should we order a second bottle of red?
Recommandons-nous une deuxième bouteille de rouge?

Can I pour you a little more wine?
Veux-tu que je te reserve un peu de vin?

Which wine do you recommend for a lamb stew?
Quel vin me recommandez-vous pour un gigot d'agneau?

I'm hosting a dinner tonight and I'm looking for some wine to go along with a seafood platter. What do you suggest?
Je tiens un dîner ce soir et je recherche un vin pour accompagner un plateau de fruits de mer. Qu'est-ce que vous me suggérez?

I'm looking for a very specific *cépage* from Languedoc-Roussillon.
Je recherche un cépage très spécifique du Languedoc-Roussillon.

What's your opinion on this Gewurztraminer?
Quelle est votre opinion sur ce Gewurztraminer?

❧ Describing wine
Décrire le vin

How would you describe this wine?
Comment décririez-vous ce vin?

What kind of wine do you like?
Quel genre de vin aimez-vous?

Positive characteristics
Caractéristiques positives

I like a wine that is...
J'aime un vin qui est...

pleasant (to drink).
aimable.

elegant / refined.
élégant / noble.

cheerful.
enjoué.

refreshing.
rafraîchissant.

connected / defined.
franc / racé.

Meaning its taste is reminiscent of its *terroir* and grapes.

full-bodied.
généreux.

mild.
léger.

A "mild" wine is lower in alcohol.

smooth / mellow.
onctueux / velouté.

full-flavored / powerful.
nerveux / puissant.

supple.
souple.

A supple wine is easy to drink and flows with ease.

Negative characteristics
Caractéristiques négatives

I can't drink wine that's...
Je ne peux pas boire du vin qui est...

This wine is too...
Ce vin est trop...

    aggressive.
    aggressif.

    acidic.
    âpre.

    reticent.
    austère.

    strong and needs to develop with age.
    austère, il a besoin de se former avec le temps.

    flat.
    plat.

    green.
    vert.

    too young.
    bourru.

Body of the wine: strengths and flaws
Le corps du vin: qualités et défauts

Taste this wine, it's very...
Goûte ce vin, il est très...

full-flavored / intense.
chaud / charnu / corsé / viril.

Intense in alcohol, warm.

balanced.
charpenté.

This wine is well-made and stable.

big / vigorous.
étoffé / ferme.

fruity.
fruité.

round.
rond.

Supple and mellow red wine.

smooth.
suave.

You don't want a wine that's...
Vous ne voulez pas d'un vin qui soit...

caustic.
acerbe.

astringent.
astringeant.

corked.
bouchonné.

flabby.
dépouillé.
An aged wine that has lost its color and flavor.

hollow.
maigre.
Lacks body and alcohol.

leathery / thick.
pâteaux.

sour.
sur.

Chapter 11

HARD ALCOHOL AND BEER

Les spiritieux et la bière

=== ❧ ===

While you most probably envision the French sipping a glass of wine on a café's *terrasse*, they also enjoy trading their favorites AOCs for some beer. Beer possesses a more down-to-earth feeling than wine, mostly because it is more affordable (and also has a lower alcohol percentage than wine). A glass of beer is mostly enjoyed during the *apéro*–meaning the beginning of the evening before going to dinner (the equivalent of *apéritif*).

The French also pride themselves with having a thick skin for liquor. Cocktails are everywhere, from chic hotels to popular bars to regular brasseries. You'll be surprised to learn how many internationally famous cocktails were actually born in France.

Alcohol
L'alcool

Beer
Bière

Benedictine
Bénédictine

This famous alcoholic beverage in France is made from spices and local plants, such as myrrh, saffron, tea, thyme, coriander, lemon, vanilla, or honey, to name a few. Counting 80 proof alcohol, it is produced in Fécamp, Normandy.

Bourbon
Bourbon

Cognac
Cognac

Gin
Gin

Pastis
Pastis

A typical alcoholic yet very sweet drink from the south of France that combines licorice with anise and is usually drunk diluted with water over ice.

Port
Porto

Rum
Rhum

Tequila
Tequila

Vermouth
Vermouth

Vodka
Vodka

Whiskey
Whisky

A bottle of vodka
Une bouteille de vodka

Beer on tap / Draft beer
Une pression

A pint of beer
Une pinte de bière

A half-pint of beer
Un demi

Lager
Une (bière) blonde

Dark beer
Une bière brune

Non-alcoholic beer
Une bière sans alcool

Can of beer
Une canette de bière

Bottle of beer
Une bouteille de bière

❖ Beer cocktails
Cocktails à base de bière

Because beer is such a common drink to enjoy after work and among friends, it was almost mandatory that cocktails would be made using this light and always-popular brew.

Le Gambetta (or Demi-Gambetta)

Le Gambetta is actually a syrup, which makes it a nonalcoholic drink, yet it is worth mentioning. Created in ancient Provence, this drink is mostly found in the south of France. Syrup is obtained through maceration of around 50 plants, fruits, and plant barks; caramel, sugar, citric acid, glucose, and fructose syrup are added as well, giving the drink a fresh and fruity flavor.

Gambetta is typically mixed with still or sparkling water, beer (to make a Demi-Gambetta), or Sprite or Seven-Up (Gambetta Limonade).

La Langue de Feu

Literally "fire tongue," this very strong cocktail is consumed in shots and composed of half vodka and half beer. It's flavored with Tabasco to give it a reddish-pink color.

Le Monaco

The Monaco is mostly known in France, Belgium, and Switzerland. A light and refreshing drink, as well as cheap, this cocktail combining beer, Sprite, Seven-Up, or other lemon-lime sodas, and grenadine syrup is quite popular in bars.

Le Panaché

The famous Panaché is a mix of Sprite and beer in varying quantities (usually, one-fourth beer and three-fourths soda). In 1979, Heineken branded the name Panach' and now sells its own ready-mixed Panaché.

Le Picon Bière

This drink was originally created by Gaétan Picon in the 19th century. After catching a fever while deployed in Algeria, he invented a mixture prepared from orange peels, quinine extract (from a medicinal plant found in South America), and gentiana scabra flowering plant (often used in Chinese medicine), all macerated in *eau-de-vie* (literally, "life water," which in French refers to distilled spirits).

Today, syrup, sugar, and caramel have been added to the concoction, and the drink is mixed with beer to create one of the most famous beverages in France: Picon Bière.

✷ Hard alcohol
Les alcools forts

The French enjoy a strong drink every now and then.

Here are the most common types of cocktails produced and consumed in France.

Un Bloody-Mary

"Bloody-Mary" typically contains vodka, tomato juice, Tabasco sauce, celery salt, Worcestershire sauce, and lemon juice. Bloody Mary is sometimes translated as the very vulgar French slang *Marie-Salope* (literally "Mary the Whore").

Le Grog

Famously known as an ancient grandma's home remedy to cure colds, Grog originally mixed rum with warm milk or hot water and some lemon and honey. Going out on Saturday night isn't the only way to enjoy a drink: You may also enjoy it stuck in bed with a flu or a sore throat—just as grandma intended.

Le mojito

One of the most preferred cocktails of the French, the mojito has a simple recipe including white rum, club soda, lime, sugar, and a dozen muddled mint leaves.

Le gin tonic

Mixing gin with tonic water, *gin tonic* is most certainly a dynamic cocktail commonly enjoyed by the French during a night out.

Le French 75

Born in 1915 in Paris's Harry's Bar, this strong French cocktail includes gin, Cointreau, lime juice, one sugar cube, and champagne.

La Margarita

A margarita is made with tequila, orange liqueur, lime juice, a slice of lime, salt, and ice cubes. The margarita has both a very tangy and powerful taste, and is commonly ordered in French bars.

Le Rose Cocktail

This drink includes French vermouth, Kirsch (cherry liqueur), and a teaspoon of strawberry syrup. It is usually enjoyed before dinner.

Kir

Originally called *blanc-cassis* (white wine with black currant liqueur), kir is a cocktail from Dijon in Burgundy that mixes

3¾ ounces white wine with ½ ounce black currant liqueur. It is enjoyed as a drink before dinner.

Many variations of the drink exist. Depending on the region you're in, either white wine is replaced by another beverage, such as red wine *(communard or cardinal)*, cider *(kir breton)*, champagne *(kir royal)*. Sometimes, black currant liqueur is replaced by another fruit liqueur, like peach *(kir à la pêche)*, blackberry *(kir à la mûre)*, or even chestnut *(kir ardéchois)*.

❀ Having a drink
Prendre un verre

We should...
Nous devrions...

> **go have a drink. It's been a long day.**
> *aller prendre un verre. Ça a été une longue journée.*

> **go celebrate with a drink!**
> *aller fêter ça avec un verre!*

> **try out this bar that makes amazing cocktails.**
> *essayer ce bar qui fait des cocktails incroyables.*

Let me...
Laisse-moi...

> **invite you for a drink.**
> *t'inviter prendre un verre.*

take you to a bar—you clearly need a drink.
t'emmener à un bar—tu as clairement besoin d'un verre.

I'd like...
J'aimerais...

to be responsible and not drink too much tonight.
être raisonnable et ne pas trop boire ce soir.

just one dry martini.
juste un dry martini.

to try this cocktail, but I'm afraid it's too strong for me.
essayer ce cocktail, mais j'ai peur qu'il ne soit trop fort à mon goût.

What are the specialties at this bar?
Quelles sont les spécialités du bar?

What cocktail would you like?
Quel cocktail voudrais-tu?

Will you have another drink?
Prendras-tu un deuxième verre?

The next round is on me!
La prochaine tournée est pour moi!

This cocktail is mind-blowing.
Ce cocktail est renversant.

TRADITIONAL FRENCH DISHES

Les plats traditionnels français

Now that you have your wines picked out, let's take a look at the dishes that so nicely complement them.

You've probably heard of dishes such as *bœuf bourguignon* or *coq au vin*, but what makes them so famous? What are the typical French dishes you are most likely to find in restaurants? Which are the ones you should absolutely taste at least once or learn to cook? Moreover, what do the French eat on Christmas or New Year's Eve? What is the *galette des rois* or the *bûche de Noël?* Let's dive into the dishes that are the heart and soul of France.

Chapter 12

TYPICAL FRENCH DISHES

Les plats typiques français

France is seen as home to timeless art, great literature, celebrated fashion, and, above all, divine food. However, some aspects of French cuisine might not be entirely attractive: The fact that the French are able to eat snails or frog legs may leave you quite perplexed, or fully disgusted. Most people in France have tasted these peculiar meals at least once, yet they don't eat them as frequently as the dishes named below.

Fortunately, France's most common dishes are exquisite and so truly French.

COMMON EXPRESSIONS
EXPRESSIONS COURANTES

Because they are so famous and commonly used, the following expressions deserve to be mentioned. Whether you're dining in the home of French friends or sitting in a restaurant, you're likely to hear them all at least once.

Bon appétit!

Literally, wishing someone a "good appetite" before a meal. This expression has become a national trademark, and it's almost mandatory to say and hear it before taking your first bite. It can also be used sarcastically when a meal turns out to not be so good-looking or tasty.

À table!

Just like saying "Dinner's ready!" This is used to call family and friends "to the table," where the meal is served.

Miam!

The equivalent to "yum!" It expresses one's delight when facing a delicious-looking meal. Children and grownups alike use it—after all, French food has a way of making you feel all childish and giggly again.

C'est bon!

To say that a meal is tasty. It's so common that the French use it as a natural response after the first bite without even thinking about it.

✺ Meat
La viande

Meat consumption may have decreased over the last 10 years in France, yet the French remain intense meat lovers. Whether it's a ham-and-butter sandwich from the bakery or *bœuf bourguignon* at a restaurant, meat is an important part of the French diet.

The following dishes are to be tasted at least once. Then you will understand just why the French love their meat so very much.

La Blanquette de veau (Normandy)

Grandmothers all over France have long delighted their grand-children with their own homemade recipes of *blanquette de veau*. It is a simple yet delicious simmered veal's breast or shoulder, cooked with carrots and onions.

The name *blanquette* contains the word *blanc* ("white"), referring to the white sauce covering the dish, made of egg yolk and cream.

A traditional recipe from Normandy, *blanquette de veau* is usually served with rice or potatoes.

Le bœuf bourguignon (Burgundy)

Originally from Burgundy—a region known for its wine and meat—the internationally famous *bœuf bourguigon* is a tradi-tional meal enjoyed during Sunday family gatherings.

It's actually a simple dish in which beef is braised in red wine and then gently cooked with mushrooms and onions to become a stew. Just like *blanquette de veau,* it can be served with carrots or potatoes. Toasted bread makes for a tasty side dish.

Le cassoulet (Languedoc-Roussillon)

A specialty from the Languedoc region in the south of France, this dish of white beans and meat—either lamb, duck, goose, or salt pork, with the possible additions of tomatoes, celery, and carrots, requires a slow-cooking technique. It's usually prepared in the morning and left simmering all day, which gives it better taste and texture.

The dish is usually served with red wine.

The name *cassoulet* dates back to the 18th century; it's based on the name of the vessel that holds the dish, an earthenware pot with slanting sides. Legend has it that *cassoulet* made its first appearance during the Hundred Years' War (1337–1453). The town of Castelnaudary was under siege from the English; on the verge of starvation, the French troops gathered their remaining food—meats and beans—and prepared a huge stew. It gave the French army enough strength to fight the English, making the dish a symbol of national pride. However, this story is only true in that the *cassoulet* is indeed an energizing dish, and it reflects once more the eternal rivalry between the French and the English.

POPULAR SAYINGS
LES EXPRESSIONS POPULAIRES

L'appétit vient en mangeant.
Literally, "appetite comes as you eat." The more you eat, the hungrier you get. So very French, indeed.

La gourmandise est un vilain défaut.
A popular saying meaning that gluttony is a flaw. It's meant to be taken lightly; for instance, you can use it to tease a friend who's about to eat both a croissant and a *financier*—before eating one of each yourself.

Avoir les yeux plus gros que le ventre.
This refers to having eyes bigger than your stomach. The problem is that it's always difficult to contain yourself, since French food offers so many appealing choices.

Avoir une faim de loup.
When you're starving, you may use the popular expression *J'ai une faim de loup*, meaning you're as hungry as a wolf.

La choucroute (Alsace)
This typical dish from eastern France is made of fermented cabbage cooked either in white wine, champagne, or hard cider. Pork products such as sausage garnish the dish.

The famous French expression *pédaler dans la choucroute* (literally, "to pedal in *choucroute*") refers to the thick texture of the dish; it's used when one has a hard time getting somewhere or getting something done.

Le civet de lièvre (Occitania)

Among the most well-known and enjoyed French meals is the *civet de lièvre*, a rabbit stew cooked with red wine, onions, herbs, shallots, and *lardons* (diced bacon). Hare is preferred over rabbit, as its flesh is more flavorful and has more character. The main characteristic that defines this dish is that the hare's blood is mixed with the red wine in the sauce.

The dish is traditionally served with the same red wine that was used to cook the stew, such as a Châteauneuf-du-Pape or a Saint-Émilion.

Le hachis parmentier (Île-de'-France)

Hachis parmentier is quite a simple dish comprising diced beef and mashed potatoes.

The name of the dish comes from Antoine Parmentier, a pharmacist and nutritionist from the 18th century who was an avid supporter of the consumption of potatoes, defending their health benefits and arguing that they could fight food shortage.

Le pot-au-feu

Pot-au-feu is another famous dish in which meat is cooked in a broth with vegetables.

Traditionally, cheap cuts of beef and cartilaginous meat such as oxtail or marrowbone are mixed with leaner cuts like rump steak or brisket and vegetables—the omnipresent carrot, celery, and onions—and spices (salt, black pepper, and cloves are among the favorites) and cooked for a long time over low heat. Ingredients can be changed in order to create different types of *pot-au-feu*.

La quiche lorraine (Lorraine)

Although originally from Germany, quiche lorraine came to France in 1605 and eventually became a French classic.

The quiche lorraine is a savory tart with a pastry crust; its filling, originally composed of cheese, has been replaced by eggs, cream, and smoked diced bacon.

Two other famous quiches exist: the *quiche vosgienne*, which adds cheese; and the *quiche alsacienne*, which includes onions.

You can order a quiche lorraine at a restaurant or find other types of quiches in bakeries. These quiche variations may include ingredients such as spinach, goat cheese, ham, and leeks.

Le Steak Tartare

Steak tartare is so famous in France that it was even mentioned in Jules Verne's novel *Michel Strogoff*. Today, the Jules Verne restaurant, famously located on the second floor of the Eiffel Tower, has made steak tartare its specialty.

In this dish, raw beef is finely chopped and garnished with Worcestershire and Tabasco sauces, salt, and pepper. Other additions include chopped shallots, cornichons, capers, parsley and a raw egg yolk. A side of french fries adds the final touch.

❊ Poultry
La volaille

Poultry comes second in the heart of the French, right after beef.

Le cordon bleu

Cordon bleu ("blue ribbon") is fried chicken breast stuffed with ham and cheese.

To make *cordon bleu*, a piece of chicken (or these days turkey) breast is slit open, filled with ham and cheese, breaded, then fried. When sliced open, the breast reveals layers of melting cheese and ham.

A *cordon bleu* also officially refers to a great chef in France; in everyday use, it refers to someone who loves to cook elaborate homemade meals.

Le confit de canard (Sud-Ouest)

The *confit de canard* is a specialty shared by the regions of Gascogne, Périgord, and Languedoc.

Seasoned pieces of duck, usually the legs, are cooked in barely simmering duck fat for hours. When cooked through, the duck is preserved in the fat, that when congealed forms a perfectly hermetic seal, allowing it to be kept for months at a time.

When needed, it is removed from the fat, then broiled or pan-fried until the meat is heated through and the skin is brown and crispy. Potatoes, cooked in the melted duck fat, and red wine accompany the dish. The cooking process involves several steps, but nowadays, every supermarket sells ready-to-cook pieces of confit.

Le coq au vin (Burgundy)

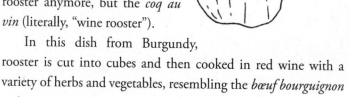

Twentieth-century French writer Gilbert Cesbron once claimed that the symbol of France was not the rooster anymore, but the *coq au vin* (literally, "wine rooster").

In this dish from Burgundy, rooster is cut into cubes and then cooked in red wine with a variety of herbs and vegetables, resembling the *bœuf bourguignon* recipe.

History has it that when Julius Caesar was conquering Gaul (in the 50s BC), an Arverni chief sent him a rooster as an act of defiance (the rooster was and is France's national symbol). Caesar invited the chief over for a feast, where he served that very rooster, cooked in wine.

❋ Fish
Le poisson

Fish may not share the popularity of meat or poultry, yet it still holds a valuable place in French cuisine as a light meal, eaten on special occasions.

Fish is also associated with Christian tradition: As a remembrance to the day Christ was born and died, it was common, notably in schools, to eat fish on Fridays.

La bouillabaisse (Provence)

Originally from Marseille, *bouillabaisse* is a seafood stew cooked in white wine and eaten with sliced bread rubbed with garlic and potatoes. The stew includes a variety of seafood, such as various varieties of Mediterranean fish, crab, and lobster, which are added to the stew in a particular order, starting with those requiring the longest cooking, down to the most delicate, fast-cooking fish.

Usually, the *bouillabaisse* is prepared for a large table. The more people there are to eat together, the better the dish.

La brandade de morue (Languedoc-Roussillon, Provence)

The *brandade de morue* is a mixture of salt cod and olive oil, to which lemon juice, garlic, parsley, and other herbs are added.

In most Parisian restaurants, the *brandade de morue* is made with milk or cream mixed with the salt cod, then browned in the oven. It is eaten by itself.

In Nîmes, the *brandade de morue* refers to a cod purée with olive oil and potatoes.

Les moules marinières (Grand-Ouest)

When going to a seaside restaurant in Normandy, be sure to order *moules marinières*. A large plate of mussels is served in *marinière* sauce, made from shallots and white wine, with a side of french fries. The dish is also famously called *moules-frites*.

✺Vegetarian dishes
Les plats végétariens

French cuisine has amazing vegetarian dishes as well, and most of them are as filling and tasty as a *blanquette de veau*. Here are the most popular:

La fondue savoyarde (Pays de Savoie)

Combining two of France's favorite ingredients—bread and cheese—*fondue savoyarde* has been enjoyed since the 17th century, especially during winter holidays.

Different types of cheese, such as Comté, Gruyère, and Emmental, are cubed then melted in a pot with white wine and a splash of liqueur; small cubes of baguette are dipped into the melted cheese, making for one of the simplest yet most delicious meals.

Le gratin dauphinois (Sud-Est)

Officially named in 1788, the *gratin dauphinois* is typically cooked for family meals.

Yellow, not-too-firm potatoes are sliced thinly and baked with crème fraîche. If cheese is added to the mixture, then it becomes a *gratin savoyard*.

La ratatouille (Provence)

A specialty from Nice dating back to the 18th century, ratatouille is a vegetable stew typically including eggplant, zucchini, peppers, and tomato with garlic, herbs, and onions, all slowly cooked in a pan. As a main dish, it is served with rice or bread, and wine.

✨ Sauces
Les sauces

Sauces are a major defining characteristic of French cuisine. Its culinary repertoire is said to count hundreds of sauces.

In the late 19th and early 20th centuries, Chef Auguste Escoffier established a list of five "mother" sauces—*béchamel, espagnole, velouté, hollandaise,* and *tomate*—which constitute the base for secondary sauces. The most common and popular sauces are:

La sauce béchamel

Although it was cook François Pierre de la Varenne who invented the sauce in the 17th century, he named it after marquis Louis de Béchameil to flatter the marquis. One of the five mother sauces, the *sauce béchamel* is a white sauce based on *roux* (a mix of butter and flour) cooked with milk or cream.

It adds something special to *croque-monsieur*, pasta with salmon, or baked ham with endive.

La sauce hollandaise

A warm sauce created under Louis XIV, hollandaise includes egg yolk, lemon juice, butter, salt, and pepper. Its appearance is yellow and opaque, while its texture is smooth and creamy. It's an especially good dip for vegetables.

La sauce tartare

One of the few spicy sauces, *sauce tartare* is made of mayonnaise, to which capers, spices, and herbs (typically chives, parsley, chervil, and tarragon) are added.

Sauce tartare goes well with fish or fried food, such as french fries.

✳ Condiments
Les condiments

Condiments are great side dishes and very much present in French cuisine. If you plan on doing some grocery shopping in France, you should know that Amora Maille is the leading producer of all condiment products—and quality products, at that.

Les cornichons

The French love their cornichons, either to introduce a course or, better, to make a sandwich. In France, pickles are typically quite small, crunchy, and tangy.

La mayonnaise (Aquitaine, Lot-et-Garonne)

Mayonnaise is so important to French cuisine that middle school students are taught how to make it in chemistry class.

A pale yellow, thick, creamy sauce, mayonnaise traces its origins back to the Balearic Islands of Spain.

Mayonnaise is a stable emulsion of egg yolk, oil, and vinegar, to which salt and pepper are added. It is almost impossible to eat boiled shrimp, french fries, or a hard-boiled egg without mayonnaise.

La moutarde de Dijon (Burgundy)

The famous *moutarde de Dijon* is a strong and spicy condiment made up of black mustard seeds, salt, and vinegar. It is a perfect pair for all types of meat.

La tapenade (Provence)

A specialty from Marseille dating back to 1880, tapenade is a purée of finely chopped olives, capers, anchovies, and olive oil.

There are two types of tapenade: black (made with black olives) and green (made with, yes, green olives). Both are great as an hors d'œuvre on crackers or toasted bread.

✹ Desserts
Les desserts

French desserts are hard to resist: not only are they aesthetically charming, but each spoonful is the most delightful experience. Whether ordering these elegant sweets at a restaurant or trying to cook them at home, there is no better way to fall in love with French cuisine than to indulge in its desserts.

La crème brûlée

Literally "burned cream," this pastry is composed of egg yolk, sugar, cream, and a rich vanilla-flavored custard base. The final touch is the top layer of hard caramel; if you have seen the movie *Amélie*, you know that one of the character's favorite things to do is to gently break the hard caramel layer with a coffee spoon.

L'île flottante

The "floating island" is a classic dessert of French cuisine. Very light, it's basically a sweetened, vanilla-tinged meringue floating on custard sauce and topped with caramel.

Le fondant au chocolat

Also called *mi-cuit* (half-cooked), the *fondant au chocolat* (*fondant* meaning "melting") is a warm chocolate cake that oozes chocolate when it comes out of the oven. Most restaurants serve it with a scoop of vanilla ice cream.

Chapter 13

FESTIVE DISHES

Les plats de fêtes

France celebrates many public holidays, some requiring specially prepared dishes. These dishes are part of old traditions, some dating back a hundred years. Here are some of the most popular celebrations *(les fêtes)*.

Happy New Year!
Bonne année!

Happy Easter!
Joyeuses Pâques!

Merry Christmas!
Joyeux Noël!

Let's toast!
Trinquons!

Cheers!
Santé! / Tchin!

❧Epiphany
Épiphanie

The French begin the new year with this hard-to-miss tradition: *la galette des rois* (the king cake). Sold in all supermarkets and bakeries during the entire month of January, this yummy, round, flaky pastry-layered cake with almond paste filling *(frangipane)* will leave you full for the whole day. A porcelain or ceramic bean *(la fève)* is hidden in the cake; whoever finds it is named king and is awarded a golden cardboard crown.

La galette des rois is usually enjoyed during family gatherings; the youngest member of the family kneels under the table and randomly designates who the slices are served to.

Dating back to the 13th century, *la galette des rois* is a Christian heritage that celebrates the day of the Epiphany, also called "Day of the Kings." It refers to the three kings, Gaspard, Balthazar, and Melchior, who came to bring the newborn Son of God gold, incense, and myrrh. The bean hidden in the *galette* traditionally portrayed the figures of the Epiphany: Jesus, Mary, the barn animals, and so on. The Blain Museum (Pays de la Loire region in Western France) is known for its collection of beans, *(fèves)* which numbers over a thousand.

You may find other types of *galettes* elsewhere in France, such as the *galette de Besançon* (a dry galette with flaky pastry layers covered with butter and sugar) or in the south of France, *gâteau des rois* (a brioche with *fruits confits*, or crystallized fruits). Here are some other useful terms.

King cake
La galette des rois

Flat puff-pastry cake
La galette

Cake
Le gâteau

Bean / Charm
La fève

Crown
La couronne

Crispy
Croustillant(e)

Plentiful
Copieux

Who...
Qui...

> **wants to cut the *galette*?**
> *veut découper la galette?*

> **will get the bean this year?**
> *obtiendra la fève cette année?*

> **is up for another slice of *galette*?**
> *est partant pour une nouvelle part de galette?*

I would like...
J'aimerais...

> **another slice of *galette*.**
> *une nouvelle part de galette.*

to get the bean and become king / queen.
obtenir la fève et devenir roi/reine.

to eat *galette* all year long.
manger de la galette toute l'année.

I bought...
J'ai acheté...

this *galette* at the bakery / the supermarket.
cette galette à la boulangerie / au supermarché.

the biggest *galette* they had.
la plus grosse galette qu'ils avaient.

all the necessary ingredients to make a *galette* from scratch.
tous les ingrédients nécessaires pour faire une galette moi-même.

❀ Candlemas
La Chandeleur

Another Christian celebration, *Chandeleur* is celebrated on February 2. That day, preparing and eating *les crêpes de la Chandeleur* is required. Why crêpes, you might ask? In the 5th century, Pope Gelasius I replaced the celebration of *Lupercales* (the celebration of purification in Ancient Rome) with *Chandeleur,* a day that celebrates light. Pope Gelasius I used to distribute crêpes to pilgrims who came to Rome; since crêpes look like solar disks, they seemed appropriate to celebrate the day of light.

Crêpe
La crêpe

Flour
La farine

Batter
La pâte

Eggs
Les œufs

Butter
Le beurre

Sugar
Le sucre

Salt
Le sel

Crêpe batter
La pâte à crêpe

Let's make crêpes for Candlemas.
Faisons des crêpes pour la Chandeleur.

Shall I serve you some crêpes?
Voulez-vous que je vous serve quelques crêpes?

What...
Que...

    would you like on your crêpes?
    veux-tu sur tes crêpes?

shall I put on your crêpes? Nutella, sugar, honey,
or jam?

*veux-tu que je mette sur tes crêpes? Du Nutella, du
sucre, du miel, ou de la confiture?*

Who wants...

Qui veut...

> **some delicious homemade crêpes?**
> *de délicieuses crêpes faites maison?*

> **the last crêpe?**
> *la dernière crêpe?*

Can I have one more crêpe, please?
Puis-je avoir une nouvelle crêpe, s'il te plaît?

Could you butter my crêpe?
Pourrais-tu beurrer ma crêpe?

 Easter
Pâques

Like many Christian countries, France celebrates Easter. Children as well as adults love it: Not only do they get to indulge in chocolate over Easter weekend, it's also a national holiday—which means on Monday, kids don't go to school and adults don't go to work.

Traditionally, chocolate *oeufs de Pâques* (Easter eggs) are hidden in the garden for children to find, and baskets are offered as gifts.

Easter eggs
Les œufs de Pâques

Chocolate eggs
Les œufs au chocolat

Gift basket
Un panier cadeau

We should...
Nous devrions...

> **hide the chocolate eggs in the garden before the kids see us.**
> *cacher les œufs au chocolat dans le jardin avant que les enfants ne nous voient.*

> **offer the neighbors a basket of chocolate eggs.**
> *offrir un panier d'œufs au chocolat aux voisins.*

❄ Christmas Eve
Le réveillon de Noël

Turkey *(La dinde)*   In France, turkey has been a regular dish served on Christmas Eve ever since the 16th century, when it was considered fancy to eat exotic animals during great feasts. Turkey, imported from the New World, was appealing because it was rarer than chicken.

Yule Log *(La bûche)*   The *bûche de Noël* is always Christmas Eve dessert.

The tradition dates back to the Middle Ages, when fruit tree logs were slowly burned in fireplaces; blessed with branches of laurel, it was meant to guarantee good harvest for the next year.

It turned into an edible dessert in the 19th century, with a loglike buttercream cake, typically frozen. The cake is found in different flavors, ranging from vanilla and chocolate to strawberry and Grand Marnier. The log is adorned with woodsy characteristics like mushrooms and axes, as well as Santa Claus and goblins.

You can buy the cakes at the supermarket in the frozen food section, but they're only available around Christmas time.

The Thirteen Desserts *(Les Treize desserts)*   In Provence, Christmas Eve dessert is not so much the *bûche* as what's called the 13 desserts. Just like the name suggests, these are 13 small desserts that are enjoyed at the end of the meal. Despite variations, they are typically *fougasse* (flatbread), candied fruits, fruit paste, *calissons* (a type of tender fruit candy), apples, pears, green melon, orange, dates, and the Four Beggars *(Les Quatre Mendiants)*. This list is not exhaustive, and depending on tastes and habits there can also be chestnuts, jam, nougat, and grapes. However, you can only have a total of 13 desserts—no more, no less.

Stuffed turkey
La dinde farcie

Yule log
La bûche de Noël

Frozen
Glacé

The Thirteen Desserts
Les Treize desserts

Figs
Les figues

Dates
Les dattes

Grapes
Les raisins

Prunes
Les pruneaux

Oranges
Les oranges

Apples
Les pommes

Pears
Les poires

Cookies
Les biscuits

Crystallized fruits
Les fruits confits

Chesnuts
Les châtaignes

Hazelnuts
Les noisettes

Walnuts
Les noix

Almonds
Les amandes

Jams
Les confitures

Fruits
Les fruits

Seasoned flatbread
La fougasse

Nougats (dark, white...)
Les nougats (noirs, blancs...)

Honey
Le miel

Green melon
Le melon vert

I would like...
J'aimerais...

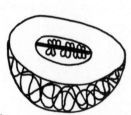

> **another slice of turkey,
> please.**
> *une autre tranche de dinde, s'il te
> plaît.*

> **dark / white meat, please.**
> *de la cuisse / du blanc, s'il vous plaît.*

> **the largest slice of yule log.**
> *la plus grosse part de bûche.*

> **to taste that delicious stuffed turkey you cooked.**
> *goûter cette délicieuse dinde farcie que tu as préparée.*

Could you...
Pourrais-tu...

> **cut me another slice of turkey?**
> *me découper une nouvelle tranche de dinde?*
>
> **take the turkey out of the oven?**
> *sortir la dinde du four?*
>
> **take the Yule log out of the freezer?**
> *sortir la bûche du congélateur?*

Shall I...
Veux-tu que...

> **serve you another slice of turkey?**
> *je te serve une nouvelle tranche de dinde?*
>
> **buy a chocolate or a strawberry Yule log?**
> *j'achète une bûche au chocolat ou à la fraise?*

❆ New Year's Eve
Le réveillon du Nouvel An

The tradition of *Les huîtres du Nouvel An* (New Year's Eve's Oysters) has been around for centuries. Oysters are bought by the dozen at the fish market in the morning; at night, they are consumed raw and accompanied, of course, by New Year's Eve champagne.

Oysters
Les huîtres

Oysters by the dozen
Les huîtres par douzaine

Oysters on the half shell
Les huîtres ouvertes

Oysters are usually served on the half shell; however, some hosts will have their guests take part in the shucking right at the table.

Bottle of champagne
Une bouteille de champagne

Could you...
Pourrais-tu...

> **help me shuck the oysters?**
> *m'aider à ouvrir ces huîtres?*

> **pour me a glass of champagne?**
> *me servir une coupe de champagne?*

Is there...
Y a t-il...

> **any champagne in the fridge?**
> *du champagne dans le frigo?*

> **anything else to eat other than oysters?**
> *autre chose à manger que des huîtres?*

I bought...
J'ai acheté...

> three dozen oysters at the fish market this
> morning.
> *trois douzaines d'huîtres chez le poissonnier ce matin.*

> two exquisite bottles of Dom Pérignon
> champagne.
> *deux bouteilles exquises de champagne Dom
> Pérignon.*

IN THE FRENCH KITCHEN

Dans la cuisine française

After moving to Paris, the soon-to-be famous chef Julia Child was told by her husband that, in France, cooking was "a combination of art form and national sport."

There couldn't be a more spot-on definition.

Yes, cooking is an art form—in fancy restaurants, your plate will look like a miniature high-fashion piece designed by Jean-Paul Gaultier, and your fork will tremble at the idea of breaking that little monument.

And yes, cooking is a national sport. In the land of culinary excellence, cheese makers to bakers, farmers to chefs strive to provide the best of their product each day; their dedication is such that their profession seems less like a job than a calling.

But first and foremost, cooking is giving. To the French, cooking for someone is the best proof of friendship or love one can show. French dishes take time and dedication to prepare, and the French are picky about eating good, homemade food. When you engage in cooking, you know this isn't a frivolous act.

Learning how to "cook French" will not only make you more aware of the techniques and details behind great dishes, it will also make you appreciate them even more.

When you cook a great dish, chances are you will have succeeded in touching the hearts of the French.

Chapter 14

THE FRENCH KITCHEN

La cuisine française

=== ❀ ===

First you will need to find your way around the French kitchen—what the typical products found in all fridges and pantries of France are and what cooking implements you'll be utilizing.

🌿 The fridge and freezer
Le frigo et le congélateur

There are certain basics that compose a French *frigo* (fridge): You are sure to find typical dairy products such as butter, cheese, yogurt, and milk (the French don't worry about getting the necessary amount of calcium each day). You'll probably also find jam and orange juice for breakfast.

Ham, pâté, and eggs are other usual inhabitants of French fridges; condiment-wise, you'll see the unavoidable mayonnaise and *moutarde*, pickles, and olives. And, of course, there will be seasonal vegetables such as greens, tomatoes, endives, and beets.

Finally, rosé and white wine can be found in the fridge.

Though the French enjoy cooking, just like anyone else, they rely on frozen food every once in awhile. Pizza, quiche, and ice cream are what you're most likely to find in any freezer.

❋ The French pantry
Le garde-manger français

A French pantry comprises the common products of olive oil, vinegar, salt, and pepper.

The necessary minimum for breakfast is there, as well: boxes of coffee and tea, honey and Nutella, cocoa powder to make chocolate milk, cereals, brioche, and loaves of bread.

When it comes to basic ingredients for cooking, you're most likely to find boxes of pasta (more popular than rice) and various cans of tuna, peas, carrots, and artichokes.

You may also come across chocolate bars and cookies for guilty pleasures, as well as flour to make crêpes among other tasty treats.

Obviously, one or two bottles of red wine always lie somewhere in the kitchen, or in the wine cellar.

✻ Cooking utensils and appliances
Ustensiles de cuisines et appareils électroménagers

When it comes to cooking—whether it's a simple quiche for yourself, a tart for a family lunch, or a cake for a friend's dinner—you'll need to master the vocabulary of kitchen utensils and appliances.

Tableware
Vaisselle et couverts

Fork
La fourchette

Salad fork
La fourchette à salade

Spoon
La cuillère

Dessert spoon
La cuillère à dessert

Teaspoon / Coffee spoon
La cuillère à café

Serving spoon
La grande cuillère

Knife
Le couteau

Cheese knife
Le couteau à fromage

Butter knife
Le couteau à beurre

Plate
L'assiette

Charger
L'assiette de présentation

Glass
Le verre

Wine glass
Le verre à vin

Champagne glass
La flûte de champagne

Kitchen utensils
Les ustensiles de cuisine

Salad servers
Les couverts à salade

Tongs
Les pinces de cuisine

Ladle
La louche

Nutcracker
Le casse-noix

Spatula
La spatule

Whisk
Le fouet

Peeler
L'éplucheur / L'économe

Apple corer
Le vide-pomme

Vegetable brush (to clean vegetables)
La brosse à légumes

Can opener
L'ouvre-boîte

Corkscrew
Le tire-bouchon

Ice cream scoop
La cuillère à glace

Ice cube tray
Le bac à glaçons

Cookware and accessories
Casseroles accessoires de cuisine

Frying pan
La poêle

Saucepan
La casserole

Skillet
Un poêlon

Stewpot
Le faitout

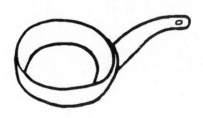

Cooking pot
La marmite

Lid
Le couvercle

Pressure cooker
La cocotte minute

Colander
La passoire

Trivet
Le dessous-de-plat

Cooking mitts
Les gants / les maniques de cuisine

Tablecloth
La nappe

Napkin
La serviette de table

Appliances
Les appareils de cuisson

Stove
La cuisinière

Stovetop
Les plaques de cuisson

Electric stovetop / Gas stovetop
Les plaques électriques / Les foyers à gaz

Range hood
La hotte aspirante

Oven
Le four

Microwave
Le micro-ondes

Refrigerator / Fridge
Le réfrigérateur / Le frigo

Dishwasher
Le lave-vaisselle

Deep-fryer
La friteuse

Toaster
Le grille-pain

Steamer
Le cuiseur à vapeur

Blender
Le mixeur

Bread maker
La machine à pain

Bread oven
Le four à pain

Electric juicer
La centrifugeuse

Manual juicer
Presse-agrume

Coffeepot / Coffee maker
La cafetière / La cafetière électrique

Teapot
La théière

Kettle
La bouilloire

Fondue set
Le service à fondue

❀ The art of setting the table
L'art de mettre la table

There might come a time when you set foot in a restaurant so fancy it's intimidating; or, when you're invited to dinner in an upper-class apartment in the very bourgeois 16th *arrondissment* (district) of Paris; or, when you simply wish to set the classiest table ever to challenge your mother-in-law's argument that you know nothing about etiquette.

Whatever the case is, you may want to learn how to hold a proper dinner—from setting the table to entertaining your guests, each detail counts, and one small error can prove fatal. Always place forks, knives, and spoons according to their use— the first fork or knife used will be placed furthest from the plate, and the last used will be closest to the plate.

Forks belong on the left side of the plate, while knives belong on the right. The sharp edge of the knife is directed toward the plate. To the right of the knives is the soup spoon.

The dessert spoon and cheese knife are placed above the plate, their handles on the right side; the cutting edge of the cheese knife should be facing the plate, while the spoon's hollow side should face downward.

Glasses are placed above the dessert spoon and cheese knife.

The water glass is placed on the left; to its right are wine glasses, which vary according to the types of wine that will be served.

Plates are positioned about an inch away from the edge of the table. It is traditional to have three plates, placed on top of one another: a charger, a dinner plate, and a shallow bowl.

The charger is removed when cheese is served.

The dinner plate sits on top of the presentation plate and is used for the main course.

The shallow bowl is the first dish you'll eat from—usually soup.

There is also a fourth plate placed apart from the others: the small bread plate. It usually rests on the upper left side of the three main plates, next to the glasses.

Napkins are the only things you have freedom over. Folded, flowerlike, on the left or right, you're free to choose how to set them—on the condition that they match your tablecloth.

※ Cooking verbs
Les verbes de cuisine

Although in French cuisine it is all about using the freshest ingredients to create delicious dishes, you also need to know how to prepare them. Following a recipe is not just reading the ingredient list and throwing everything together—it takes precision and discipline, as well as a wide vocabulary. Here's a list of words you might find helpful when going through a recipe's instructions.

Cooling
Refroidir

> **To cool**
> *Refroidir*
>
> **To freeze**
> *Glacer / Congeler*
>
> **To preserve**
> *Conserver*

TABLE ETIQUETTE
LES MANIÈRES À TABLE

Setting the table is, however, not enough: You have to learn the proper manners. In fact, having lunch or dinner implies following certain etiquette.

- Never put your elbows on the table: Such posture is far from elegant.
- Don't salt your food before taking a bite—you could upset the chef.
- Although it is delicious, avoid sopping up any extra sauce left on your plate with a piece of bread.
- Never cross your knife and fork on your plate when you're done. Instead, place them parallel to each other; it doesn't matter which way they are facing
- Finally, be the best of hosts by creating a friendly atmosphere for your guests. Introduce everyone to each other at the beginning, make sure everyone feels included in the conversation, and try to avoid topics like politics and money, unless you know your guests are reasonable people and won't turn dinner into a food fight.

Cutting
Couper

To cut
Découper

To chop finely
Ciseler

A small dice, especially when referring to onions, shallots, and fragile herbs like basil or chives.

To chop
Hacher

When used for meat, it means to grind (in a machine) or to chop finely like for steak tartare.

To slice
Effiler / Trancher

To cut thinly into rounds
Émincer

To grate
Râper

To peel
Éplucher

Heating
Réchauffer

To bake
Cuire au four

To boil
Bouillir

To blanch
Ebouillanter / Blanchir

To braise
Braiser

To bread
Paner

To broil
Griller

To brown
Dorer / Rissoler

To brew
Infuser

To cook
Cuisiner / Faire la cuisine

To flambé
Flamber

To fry
Frire

To heat / Reheat
Chauffer / Réchauffer

To macerate
Macérer

To marinate
Mariner

To melt
Fondre

To roast
Rôtir

To simmer
Mijoter

To steam
Cuire à la vapeur

To stuff
Farcir

To toast
Griller

To warm up
Réchauffer

MEAT COOKING PREPARATIONS
LES TYPES DE CUISSON DE VIANDE

Rare
Bleu

Medium
A point

Medium-rare
Saignant

Well-done
Bien-cuit

Handling food
Préparer les ingrédients

To beat
Battre

To blend
Mélanger

To grease
Graisser

To fill
Fourrer

To flatten
Aplatir

To fold (in)
Incorporer

To knead
Travailler

To mix
Mixer

To roll out
Abaisser

To stir
Remuer

To whisk
Fouetter

Seasoning
Assaisonner

To baste
Arroser

To butter
Beurrer

To dress
Habiller

To dust with sugar
Saupoudrer de sucre

To flour
Fariner

To garnish
Garnir

To oil
Huiler

To pepper
Poivrer

To salt
Saler

To season
Assaisonner

To spice
Pimenter

To sprinkle
Saupoudrer

To top
Couvrir

Methods of cooking
Les méthodes de cuisson

Braised
À l'étouffée / Braisé

Breaded
Pané

Confit
Confit

Over a double-boil
Au bain-marie

Fried
Frit

Ground (meat)
Haché

Half-cooked
Mi-cuit

Raw
Cru

Roasted
Rôti

Sautéed / Pan sautéed
Sauté / à la Poêle

Smoked
Fumé

Steamed
À la vapeur

Stuffed
Farci

Well-cooked
À point

Miscellaneous
Divers

To turn on
Allumer

To turn on the gas burners
Allumer le gaz

To turn off
Eteindre

To preheat the oven
Mettre le four à chauffer

To cook something
Mettre quelque chose à cuire / Faire cuire quelque chose

To cook over low heat
Faire cuire à feu doux

Chapter 15

RECIPES

Les recettes

So far, you have discovered how important eating is in France—eating not only quality food, but making time for it. And because there's no eating without cooking, you should now be introduced to the latter. Despite the fact that some dishes have been in existence for a hundred years, mastering their recipes requires great skill, knowledge, and dedication. And the most simple-looking recipes will harbor details and ingredients of the utmost importance. When you know which secrets lie behind some dishes, you'll come to appreciate their unique taste even more than before. Yet, the most important reason why you need to learn or improve your French cooking skills is that then you're sure to succeed in touching the hearts of the French.

Now, roll up your sleeves and tie your apron: The time has come for you to master French cuisine.

❀ Sauces
Les sauces

La sauce béchamel

A major sauce in French cuisine, béchamel sauce is not
only easy to prepare, but it will make your dishes with
fish or eggs taste even more delicious.   SERVES 6

3 tablespoons butter

3 tablespoons flour

½ liter (2 cups) milk

salt and pepper

In a saucepan make the *roux:* melt the butter over low heat.
Add the flour and stir gently until the mixture becomes
foamy.

Gradually add the milk, then season with salt and pepper.
Stir until it gets thick—about 5 minutes.

La sauce tartare

If there is only one sauce you should master, it is
sauce tartare. This classic French sauce will take any
dish of yours to the next level.   SERVES 6

3 eggs, hard boiled

2 teaspoons mustard

400 milliliters (1⅔ cups) olive oil

8 finely chopped cornichons

3 teaspoons minced fresh parsley or tarragon

1 teaspoon minced capers

2 teaspoons lemon juice or wine vinegar

salt and pepper

Peel the eggs and separate the egg whites from the yolks.
Mash the egg whites with a fork and set aside.

Place the yolks in a large bowl and whisk them with the
mustard. Season with salt and pepper, then add the olive
oil, gradually, drop by drop at first, then in a drizzle, and
whisk to combine. Add the vinegar and whisk until you get a
homogeneous mixture.

Add the diced cornichons, parsley or tarragon, capers, and
egg whites. Gently whisk the whole mix. Refrigerate for
about 2 hours before serving.

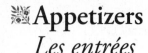
Les tomates à la provençale

In the sunny and warm south of France, dishes were made to be light and fresh, just like the tomato-based dish *tomates à la provençale*. Great as an appetizer, they'll pair best with a Rosé Côtes de Provence.   SERVES 6

6 ripe tomatoes (900 grams / 2 pounds)

600 milliliters (2½ cups) olive oil

20 grams (1 ounce) dried breadcrumbs

2 teaspoons minced fresh basil

2 teaspoons minced fresh parsley

3 cloves garlic, minced

salt and pepper

Preheat the oven to 200°C (400°F).

Cut the tomatoes in half lengthwise and carve out the seeds and core with a spoon and discard. Place the tomato halves in a gratin dish.

Put the rest of the ingredients in a medium bowl and mix together. Fill the tomatoes with the mixture. Drizzle the olive oil on the tomatoes. Bake for 15 to 20 minutes. The tomatoes should look warm and melted a little.

La soupe à l'oignon

This regional dish from Alsace (eastern France) is usually consumed in winter to warm up. Onion soup requires 20 minutes of preparation and one hour of cooking, but you'll see that the taste you achieve makes it worth your time. To make your dish even more delicious, pair it with a Beaujolais or Riesling.   SERVES 6

    1 kilogram (2 pounds) thinly sliced onion

    4 teaspoons (20 milliliters) olive oil

    1.5 liters (6⅓ cups) beef or chicken broth

    bread, for serving

    100 grams (4 ounces) grated Gruyère

    salt and pepper

In a large saucepan or casserole, place the onions and olive oil. Season with salt and pepper, then gently stir occasionally over medium-low heat for about 20 minutes.

Slowly add the beef or chicken broth and keep stirring. Cook for 20 minutes more.

Ladle soup into oven-proof bowls, top each bowl with a slice of bread, cover with the grated cheese and broil until the cheese is browned.

❊Meat
La viande

Le veau marengo

Like most great dishes, *veau marengo* requires dedication and time.
Your guests will be sure to thank you when they taste this delicious
veal broth alongside potatoes or pasta and either Rosé de Provence,
Bordeaux rouge Supérieur, Côtes du Rhône, or Chablis.   SERVES 6

40 milliliters (3 tablespoons) olive oil, divided

1.3 kilograms (2½ pounds) veal shoulder, cubed

handful of fresh basil

handful of fresh thyme

2 medium onions, minced, divided

40 grams (⅓ cup) flour

500 milliliters (2 cups) dry white wine

230 grams (½ pound) button mushrooms, quartered

2 carrots, diced

450 grams (1 pound) firm tomatoes, peeled and unseeded;
cut into 4

salt and pepper

In a dutch oven, heat 2 tablespoons of the olive oil over
medium heat, then place the veal cubes in the pan. Stir the
pieces regularly until the meat has browned evenly. Add
the basil, thyme and half of the onion. Add the flour and stir
over medium heat. The flour should turn blond-colored.

Add the white wine, carrots, mushrooms, and remaining onion. Cook for 5 minutes.

Finally, add the tomatoes, and season with salt and pepper to taste. Cover and let simmer for about an hour over low heat.

Les paupiettes de bœuf

While you may also find paupiettes of veal or pork, *paupiettes de bœuf* (from the Italian *polpetta*, "meatball") unconditionally remains one of the most popular dishes in France. You can enhance the unique flavor of *paupiettes de bœuf* by serving red wine, such as Bordeaux rouge, Beaujolais, Languedoc rouge, or Côtes-du-Rhône.   SERVES 6

  2 teaspoons butter

  1 onion, sliced

  4 slices rumpsteak (1 kilogram / 2 pounds)

  230 grams (½ pound) smoked lardons (diced bacon)

  2 teaspoons flour

  1 (750 milliliters) bottle red wine

  bunch of thyme

  1 stalk celery

  bunch of parsley

  bunch of rosemary

  3 cloves garlic, divided

  230 grams (½ pound) button mushrooms

  2 teaspoons olive oil

  salt and pepper

ADDITIONAL EQUIPMENT:

kitchen twine

In a frying pan, heat the butter with the sliced onion over high heat. Season with salt and pepper. Stir until onion slices are cooked, about 10 minutes.

Spread cooked onions on each slice of flattened rumpsteak. Wrap the slices around the onions and tie each one firmly with kitchen string. They should now look like plump little bundles.

Place the smoked lardons in a large pan or casserole over medium heat. When they are firm-looking, place your paupiettes in the pan. Cook until slightly browned. Add the flour and stir, pour in the red wine, then add the bouquet garni and garlic.

Cover and let it simmer for one hour over low heat.

Meanwhile, cook the mushrooms over medium heat in a frying pan with the olive oil. Season with salt and pepper. When the paupiettes have been cooking for an hour, pour the mushrooms into the pan and cook again for about 10 minutes over medium heat. Serve warm.

✳Chicken
Le poulet

La fricassée de poulet

A typical dish from the region of Poitou in western France, chicken
fricassée will make you experience chicken in a whole new way. Try
a red wine from Bordeaux or Saint-Chinian, a Rosé de Provence,
or a white wine from Vouvray with this dish.   SERVES 6

> 1 onion
>
> 4 shallots
>
> 1 large tomato, peeled
>
> 4 teaspoons (20 milliliters) olive oil
>
> 1 whole chicken (1.5 kilograms / about 3 pounds),
> cut into 6 pieces
>
> salt and pepper

Cut the onion and shallots into four pieces each and chop
the tomato into a small dice. In a large, deep frying pan, heat
the olive oil over medium heat, then brown the chicken
pieces. Season with salt and pepper.

Remove the chicken pieces from the pan and add the
onions and shallots. Cook until they are slightly browned,
then return the chicken pieces to the pan. Stir, then add the
tomato.

Pour the water over the whole pan. Cover and cook over
medium-low heat for about an hour, stirring regularly.

Le poulet à l'estragon

This dish is very easy to make and pairs chicken with tarragon, creating an interesting and appealing marriage of flavors. *Poulet à l'estragon* is usually served with rice or potatoes. As for wine, opt for Chablis, Puilly Fuissé, Meursault, Vouvray, or Rosé de Provence.   SERVES 6

> 1 whole chicken (1.5 kilograms / about 3 pounds), cut into 6 pieces
>
> 30 milliliters (2 tablespoons) olive oil
>
> 4 sprigs fresh tarragon
>
> salt and pepper

Preheat the oven to 190°C (375°F).

Place the chicken pieces in an oven-safe dish. Drizzle with the olive oil, garnish with the tarragon, and season with salt and pepper. Bake for about 40 minutes. Turn the chicken pieces every 10 to 15 minutes so that all sides are evenly browned.

Serve warm.

Fish
Le poisson

La sole meunière

You'll be delighted by this specialty from Normandy: fillet of sole in butter sauce. Pair this dish with potatoes or rice, and serve with a Riesling, Chablis, Sancerre, or other dry white wine. SERVES 6

6 sole fillets (about 230 grams / ⅓ to ½ pound each)

3 tablespoons flour

3 teaspoons salted butter, divided

juice of 1 lemon

10 sprigs fresh parsley, stems removed and leaves thinly sliced

salt and pepper

Remove the skin from the sole fillets. Season the fillets with salt and pepper.

Spread the flour on a plate and individually dredge both sides of each fillet, shaking each one to remove any excess flour.

Melt 1 tablespoon of the butter in a large frying pan over medium heat. Place one fillet (or two, if you have space) in the frying pan and cook over low heat for 5 minutes. Turn over the fillet and leave it to cook for another 5 minutes. Repeat with additional butter and the remaining sole fillets.

Season the cooked fish with lemon juice and parsley to serve.

La truite aux amandes

This simple yet tasty dish was born in the Loire region in the center of France. It is especially sure to please almond lovers. *Truite aux amandes* pairs well with rice and potatoes, and a Chardonnay or Pouilly Fumé.   SERVES 6

100 grams (1 cup) flour

2 fresh trout; whole and cleaned

50 grams (¼ cup / ½ stick) butter

100 grams almonds (3 ounces)

salt and pepper

Spread the flour on a plate and individually dredge both sides of each fish, shaking each one to remove any excess flour.

In a frying pan, melt the butter over medium-low heat and then brown the trout for 10 minutes. Turn the fish over and cook for another 5 minutes.

In a separate frying pan, toast the almonds whole over very low heat with the butter. Watch them closely, stirring until they are evenly browned.

Remove the trout and season with salt and pepper. Sprinkle with almonds and serve.

Vegetarian
Végétarien

Le gratin savoyard

This regional dish from Rhône-Alpes has been enjoyed all over France for centuries. It's a dish most grandmothers will cook on Sundays when their families are over. Even better with a glass of red wine from Bordeaux or Beaujolais Villages.   SERVES 6

- 1 kilogram (2 pounds) white potatoes
- 1 or 2 cloves garlic, minced
- 500 milliliters (2 cups) milk
- 50 grams (¼ cup / ½ stick) butter
- 400 milliliters (1½ cups) whipping cream
- 160 grams (5 ounces) Gruyère, grated
- salt and pepper

Preheat the oven to 180°C (350°F) and butter a gratin dish.

Peel the potatoes, wash, and slice as thinly as possible, (about ⅛-inch thick).

In a saucepan, combine the milk and garlic, and season with salt and pepper. Bring to a boil. Once the milk is boiling, add the potatoes. Cook for about 10 minutes. Transfer the warm mixture into the prepared gratin dish. Pour the cream on top and sprinkle with the grated cheese. Bake for about an hour, until the top is golden brown.

La ratatouille

It's no surprise an animated movie was based on this popular dish from Provence: ratatouille, indeed, is exquisite. The recipe below is just one of the many ways to cook ratatouille. The dish may be served hot or cold, as is, or paired with rice or bread. Opt for a Rosé des Côtes de Provence for the greatest flavors.   SERVES 6

2 eggplants, peeled and diced

2 zucchini, sliced 30 milliliters (2 tablespoons) olive oil

2 onions, peeled and sliced

2 cloves garlic, sliced

1 red bell pepper, seeded and quartered

1 yellow bell pepper, seeded and quartered

bunch of parsley, finely chopped

bunch of rosemary, finely chopped

5 ripe and firm tomatoes, cut into 8 pieces each

salt and pepper

Heat the olive oil in a large pan or casserole over medium heat, then add the eggplant, zucchini, onion, garlic, and peppers. Cook for 5 minutes, then add the herbs. Stir, then add the tomatoes. Season with salt and pepper.

Cook over gentle heat for 20 to 30 minutes, stirring regularly.

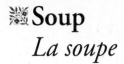 # Soup
La soupe

La soupe de cresson

If you love soup, you'll be enchanted by watercress soup; if you aren't quite a soup lover, you'll be surprisingly pleased by this famous dish from the north of France.   SERVES 6

- 1 teaspoon butter
- 1 shallot, minced
- 1 small bunch tarragon
- 2 bunches watercress, trimmed and chopped
- 1 liter (4 cups) water
- 80 milliliters (⅓ cup) whipping cream
- salt and pepper

Melt the butter in a large pan or casserole over medium heat. Add the shallot and cook until softened, then add the tarragon and watercress. Season with salt and pepper, and cook, stirring, for about 5 minutes.

Pour the water into the pan and bring to a boil over high heat. Remove from the heat.

Purée the vegetables with an immersion blender. Place back on the stovetop over low heat.

Add the whipping cream and stir until fully incorporated, about 5 minutes.

Serve warm.

La soupe de cerise

A traditional dish from Alsace that can be
enjoyed all year long.   SERVES 6

800 grams (1¾ pounds) red cherries

3 glasses red wine (ideally Bordeaux)

3 teaspoons sugar

2 cinnamon sticks

Rinse the cherries and remove the stems and pits.

In a large pan or casserole, bring the red wine to a boil with
the sugar and cinnamon sticks. Reduce the heat to medium
and add the cherries. Cook for 5 minutes.

Pour the soup into a heat-safe bowl. Refrigerate for several
hours or overnight.

Serve chilled.

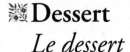

Dessert
Le dessert

Le gâteau basque

This specialty from Pays Basque in southwestern France is a thick pie with a delicate lemon flavor. Enjoy *gâteau basque* with a typical dessert wine, such as the sweet Jurançon white.   SERVES 6

FOR THE DOUGH

50 grams (¼ cup / ½ stick) unsalted butter, at room temperature

60 grams (5 tablespoons) granulated sugar

¼ teaspoon vanilla extract

2 eggs

250 grams (2 cups) flour

1 teaspoon salt

1 teaspoon baking powder

FOR THE FILLING

250 milliliters (1 cup) milk

¼ teaspoon vanilla extract

2 teaspoons sugar

2 egg yolks

25 grams (¼ cup) flour

powdered sugar, for sprinkling

½ cup almond flour

FOR THE EGG WASH

1 whole egg

PREPARING THE DOUGH: In a large mixing bowl, first whisk the butter with the sugar and vanilla. Then add the eggs, flour, salt, and baking powder, and whisk until the mixture turns into a thick dough.

Gently knead the dough with your hands and roll it until it forms a ball. Let it rest in the refrigerator for at least 1 hour.

PREPARING THE CREAM: In a small saucepan over high heat, allow the milk and vanilla to come to a boil.

In a bowl, whisk the sugar and egg yolks; add the flour, whisking continuously. Gradually pour the warm milk mixture into in the bowl and whisk vigorously. Pour the mixture back into the saucepan and stir over low heat. The cream should pull away from the sides of the saucepan.

Pour the cream into a heat-safe bowl, and stir in powdered sugar. Let the cream cool a little.

ASSEMBLING THE CAKE: Preheat the oven to 200°C (400°F).

Butter a round cake tin. Use two-thirds of the dough to cover the bottom of the tin and the sides by pushing it into the pan with your fingers. Fill it with the cream and almond flour on top of the cream. Then spread the rest of the dough on top so that it covers the entire pan.

Beat the whole egg in a small bowl and brush it over the cake.

Bake the cake for 45 minutes or until it is golden brown.

Let it cool before serving.

L'île flottante

A very light and cold dessert found in most restaurants. Very easy to prepare, you'll enjoy making it as much as you'll love eating it. Demi-sec/champagne, Sauternes, Gewurztraminer, or other sweet white wine will best match with this treat.   SERVES 6

FOR THE CUSTARD SAUCE
500 milliliters (2 cups) milk

1 vanilla bean

4 eggs

20 grams (5 teaspoons) sugar

FOR THE BEATEN EGG WHITES
2 teaspoons sugar

FOR THE CARAMEL
50 grams (4 tablespoons) sugar

PREPARING THE CUSTARD SAUCE: In a small saucepan, bring the milk with the vanilla bean to a boil over medium heat. Once it comes to a boil, turn off the heat. Let the vanilla infuse for 5 minutes, then remove the bean from the milk.

Separate the egg whites from the yolks. Set the whites aside. Whisk the egg yolks with the sugar. Then add the egg yolk mixture to the milk and cook over low heat for about 10 minutes. Stir gently. Transfer the mixture to a heat-safe bowl and let cool to room temperature in a bowl.

PREPARING THE BEATEN EGG WHITES: Beat the egg whites with the sugar until stiff peaks form. Bring a few inches of water to a boil in a saucepan. With a teaspoon, form medium balls of the beaten egg whites and cook them on the surface of the boiling water for 1 minute.

When cooked, drain with a slotted spoon; place the white balls on top of the custard sauce in the bowl.

PREPARING THE CARAMEL: In a small saucepan, cook the sugar over low heat, stirring, until the sugar has fully dissolved. Once the sugar has dissolved, let cook for several minutes until the desired color and consistency are reached. The color should range from a light golden brown to a darker copper. Be careful not to burn the caramel. As soon as desired color is reached, remove from heat and drizzle over the egg whites. Serve immediately.

Acknowledgments

I first and foremost thank Alice Riegert for guiding me through this culinary journey. Her constant support and advice have helped me make this book better each time.

I also thank Keith Riegert for believing in me and Ulysses Press for giving me the wonderful opportunity to write this book.

Most importantly, I thank my mother for teaching me to appreciate food and value its importance, and for trusting in me.

About the Author

A French native, **Victoria Mas** was raised in the south of France and fed unique local specialties from her village that still haunt her today.

After studying in California, she got her master's degree in literature from the Paris Sorbonne University and remembers all the times she stepped into her favorite Montmartre bakery to get through the exams. A compulsive reader and croissant eater, she has worked as a cultural columnist, a photographer, and a screenwriter and writer for various projects in film, theater, and TV. She is devoted to writing and sharing her passion for French food with which, like all her compatriots, she's had a romance since childhood.